Inside the Cloistered Life

SR. MARIE OF THE TRINITY

INSIDE *the* CLOISTERED LIFE

Personal Letters of a Carmelite Nun

SOPHIA INSTITUTE PRESS

Manchester, New Hampshire

Sophia Institute Press
Box 5284, Manchester, NH 03108
1-800-888-9344
www.SophiaInstitute.com

Sophia Institute Press® is a registered trademark of Sophia Institute.

paperback ISBN 979-8-88911-098-9

ebook ISBN 979-8-88911-099-6

Library of Congress Control Number: 2024936651

First printing

We humbly offer this simple little book
to show our love for
our Immaculate Mother, the Queen of Carmel,
and to give all its readers a more complete knowledge
of the daughters of the glorious
St. Teresa of Ávila, our holy Mother.

Feast of St. Teresa of Ávila
October 15, 1956

Contents

Foreword to the 1957 Edition

UNDER THE ETERNAL DESIGNS OF God, His glory and the salvation of souls is effected by the redeeming acts of Christ and all the prayers and good works of the members of Christ's Body, His Church. We glorify God and are able to save our souls by union with Christ through grace, and this union with Christ establishes a union with all men: "We being many, are one body in Christ, and every one members one of another" (Rom. 12:5).

By virtue of the character of Baptism and Confirmation, every Christian has the calling to glorify God and to work for the salvation of his own soul and that of others through Christ.

By virtue of her special vocation, the Carmelite Nun undertakes the duty of a special devotion to the glory of God, and to the salvation of her own soul and that of others. She does so by endeavoring to devote all of her time and talent to a lofty spirit of prayer, self-denial, penance, and good works. Every activity of the cloister is directed in a special way to the apostolate of souls.

In leaving the world, the Carmelite Nun does not forget the world but remembers it in prayer, sacrifice, and penance. Hers is not a life of leisure. Her days are very busy days, filled with constant activities.

Prayer holds primacy in the apostolate for souls that, after the glory of God, is the special vocation of the Carmelite Nun. St. Paul referred to Our Lord as living always to make intercession for us (Heb. 7:25). The Carmelite spends her entire life to keep her mind and heart in oneness with Christ in this constant prayer of intercession for us. In keeping with the *Rule* of Carmel, she spends her time "watching in prayer, unless otherwise justly employed."

In addition to prayer, the vocation of the Carmelite Nun requires the practice of good works and penance. St. Paul prays that every Christian "may know him [Christ] ... and the fellowship of his sufferings, being made conformable to his death" (Phil. 3:10). One of the glories of Carmel is the fact that the Carmelite Nun has the holy vocation to fill up what is wanting in the works of penance and reparation for the sins of men. All the powers and faculties of the Carmelite are mortified under the vows of poverty, chastity, and obedience, and under the *Rule* of Carmel she daily undertakes an unbroken life of fasting, abstinence, and other penitential practices. The fruits of this life of penance and reparation become the common property of the members of Christ's Body, the Church, and are directed in a special way for the good of those who are close to Carmel.

In her book *A Few Lines to Tell You*,[1] Sister Marie describes in detail the life of a Carmelite Nun and shows us by what means and in what manner rich spiritual treasure is being gathered for the benefit of all of us at the Carmel of the Holy Cross. When this Carmel was established in Iron Mountain, Michigan, in 1951, we welcomed it with a prayer that it would bring abundant fruit for

---

[1] The original title of this book when it was first published in 1957 was *A Few Lines to Tell You: My Life in Carmel.*

the glory of God and the salvation of souls in our midst. We are confident that our prayer was answered.

We pray that Sister Marie's book will serve to strengthen the holy purposes of every nun at Mount Carmel, and that it will serve to bring the faithful who read it closer to Mount Carmel. We pray, dear reader, that this book will make you realize more than ever that the Carmel of the Holy Cross is your Mount Carmel.

Thomas L. Noa, Bishop of Marquette
Feast of the Immaculate Conception
Marquette, Michigan

Preface to the 2024 Edition

THE AUTHOR OF THESE LETTERS, writing under the pseudonym of Sister Marie of the Trinity, was Sister Claire Marie of the Immaculate Heart, O.C.D. (1925–1996). Sister Claire Marie, as a young Carmelite, was part of the small group of nuns that set out from the Carmel in Grand Rapids, Michigan, in 1951 to make the new foundation in Iron Mountain, Michigan. In order to introduce the Carmelite life to the people of the Marquette Diocese, Sister wrote a series of "letters home" that were published in the diocesan newspaper. This series met with a positive reception, and so the letters were eventually put together as a book in 1957 bearing the title *A Few Lines to Tell You.*

As we reread these pages today, it is uplifting to see the continuity of spirit within our Carmelite community linking us to our beloved founding Mothers and Sisters. Decades later, so many of our cherished customs and practices endure as we strive to live our life of love, prayer, and sacrifice for the Church and for her pastors as envisioned by St. Teresa of Jesus for her daughters.

Necessarily, some changes have been made over time, required by various legislations issued by the Holy See and by the documents of the Second Vatican Council. As St. Teresa herself would desire, we have always striven to be "true daughters of the Church" as she was, always careful to safeguard the essentials of our cloistered Carmelite vocation. The letters in this book, written in the 1950s, have been left as they came from Sister Claire Marie's pen, but the changes introduced over the years have been indicated in footnotes.

We were humbly delighted to learn that Sophia Press wished to reprint our little book and hope that it continues to help make our Carmelite life known. We here wish to assure each one of its readers a special remembrance in the prayers and sacrifices of the Nuns of the Carmel of the Holy Cross in Iron Mountain, Michigan. If any young woman feels the desire to embrace this beautiful vocation, our contact information is given below:

The Discalced Carmelite Nuns
Monastery of the Holy Cross
P.O. Box 397
Iron Mountain, MI 49801
(906) 774-0561
e-mail: vocation@holycrosscarmel.com

Acknowledgments

MAY GOD REWARD AND BLESS all those who have encouraged and helped us publish this little book: especially our Very Reverend Father Albert of the Blessed Sacrament, O.C.D., and Father Edward, O.C.D., for the advice so kindly given; our loved sisters of the Carmel of the Holy Spirit, Littleton, Colorado, for assisting us with the illustrations; and Sister Mary Jerome, R.S.M., principal of Cathedral High School, Pittsburgh, Pennsylvania, for correcting the manuscript.

The Discalced Carmelite Nuns
Carmel of the Holy Cross
Iron Mountain, Michigan

Introduction to the 1957 Edition

CARMEL—THE VERY WORD IS MUSIC to our ears and evokes in every Christian mind the holiest of thoughts and memories. It is closely associated with Mary, the Mother of God, and makes us think of her because one of her most ancient and beloved titles is "Our Lady of Mount Carmel."

Mount Carmel, the mountain sentinel of the Holy Land, protects the treasures found in the interior of this land chosen by God Himself. It is a fertile region, and this mountain is one of the most noble in Palestine. In spring, it is crowned with choice flowers and, in sharp contrast with the other mountains of Judea, preserves its viridity throughout the year. Is it any wonder, then, that in the inspired Word of God we find the Spouse described in these words: "Thy head is like Carmel" (Song of Sol. 7:5); that is, beautiful, fair, and lovely? And who is this Spouse? None other than the Blessed Virgin Mary, who rises high above all other women in beauty of soul and body like a beautiful and majestic mountain. Mary, ever-fruitful Virgin crowned with all the flowers of every virtue, is like Carmel—"Thy head is like Carmel."

As Carmel is more eminent in its beauty, charm, and fruitfulness than the other mountains of Judea, the Spouse of God, Mary most holy, in a similar manner excels all other women because of the beauty of her divine maternity. Carmel, in a certain manner, is an image of the Blessed Virgin, because it is a mountain of flowers and continual fruitfulness, and it depicts the Spouse of God Mary—clothed with every virtue and grace to charm the Heart of God.

This holy mountain brings to our minds Elias,[2] the prophet of God, who "stood up as a fire, and his word burnt like a torch" (Sir. 48:1), for he walked in the presence of the living God bearing witness that the Lord God of Hosts is the only true God. Carmel speaks to us of the power of God who, because of the prayer of Elias, caused fire to descend from Heaven and consume the sacrifice he was offering in order to prove conclusively to the idolators that He was the true God and the only God to be served and adored.

And Carmel speaks to us of the power of prayer because it was on this holy mountain that Elias prayed during an extended drought so that the floodgates of Heaven were opened, and rain fell on the parched earth to renew the richness of life and bring fertility to a barren land. Carmel thus speaks to us of prayer, of divine contemplation, of closeness to God, and of intense and great familiarity with Him.

The beauty of Carmel continues to be revealed and reflected throughout the centuries, for when we speak of Carmel in the present day, we think of Teresa of Ávila: an eagle who soared to the heights of perfection and union of soul with God, and who was granted an amazing degree of intimacy with the Almighty. Teresa is one of those sovereign souls created from time to time by Almighty God seemingly so that He might show us what the human race was originally created for and to what heights, with

---

[2] Elijah in modern Bible translations.

the help of His grace, it can still attain. Teresa renewed the ancient beauty of Carmel and gave added luster to it.

Carmel brings to our minds St. John of the Cross with his doctrine of the absolute, which leads souls to divine union and wherein the soul reflects the beauty of God and sees itself in God's beauty. This saint sings a spiritual canticle, revealing the beauty of Carmel by his contemplation of divine things and by his soul burning with love—love that becomes a living flame!

"Neither roses nor lilies are wanting"[3] in the adornment of Carmel, for in our time, this holy name calls to every mind the beauty of a rose—St. Thérèse of the Child Jesus—who attained a wondrous love of God, walking in trust and simplicity by her little way of spiritual childhood.

And at the present moment, Carmel speaks to us of a heroic army of cloistered women who offer their services to God in a life of silence and obscurity in order to obtain graces for the sanctification of priests and conversion of sinners. This heroic army of chosen souls has become the greatest order of cloistered women in the Church, whose members use the means of austerity, silence, retirement, and continual prayer to attain consummate perfection of the interior life.

These daughters of the valiant Teresa of Ávila, the Discalced Carmelite Nuns, have crossed the oceans without fear, have penetrated the jungles without trepidation, and have shed their blood for Christ in order that souls might be saved and sanctified. The chosen members of the army of the Blessed Virgin and daughters of Teresa have not hesitated to go throughout the entire world and, despite hardships and privations, generously offered themselves for the salvation of souls.

---

[3] Carmelite Liturgy, *Festum Sanctorum Omnium O. N.*, November 14.

Inside the Cloistered Life

This introduction will bring you to the pages of a book that will give you an intimate view of the life of the Discalced Carmelite Nuns and a deep insight into their spirit. In this book, you will be able to follow them very closely in their great role as "mothers of souls," and you will be able to accompany them in their work for the Church and in their ascent to the summit of the mount of perfection.

The Discalced Carmelite Nuns show forth in their lives the perennial beauty of Carmel—which is only a faint reflection of the beauty of the Mother of God, Mary, Our Lady of Mount Carmel.

Father Albert of the Blessed Sacrament, O.C.D.
Feast of the Immaculate Heart of Mary
Holy Hill

Inside the Cloistered Life

Letter One

*D*earest Mother and Dad,

A Carmelite, at last, thanks be to God!

You are probably most anxious to know every detail of the trip. Never will words express the feelings I experienced as that train pulled out of Union Station and I watched the sparkling lights of the city fade from sight. Leaving the family, friends, and even the city I loved not just for a space of time but forever caused even unemotional me to feel some heart-tugs. I confess, if human respect had not dictated a more prudent course of action, I should have pulled the buzzer, stopped the train, and returned right home. Is it not wonderful how God uses even our self-love to get us through trying times?

Well, a night on a Pullman[4] never was meant to be a restful experience. Morning finally dawned, and the daylight put new life in my somewhat homesick spirits. A good breakfast put the finishing touch to bolstering my morale. Between watching the unfamiliar level landscape and writing little farewell notes to all my girlfriends, I was kept so busy that the time sped by. A change

---

[4] A railroad sleeping car.

of trains in the big Chicago station then put me en route to Iron Mountain.

One funny occurrence might interest you. We stopped for about ten minutes once, during which time the train was split, going to a different engine with an entirely different destination. I happened to be off the train when the porter announced the change; so when the train started and the porter saw me seated in the same spot, he said, "Lady, where are you going?" "Iron Mountain," I replied. "Glory be!" he exclaimed. "You're on the wrong train!" So he stopped that train; signaled across the yards to stop the other train, just pulling out; and sent me running after the departing coach. What a spectacle that made for all the passengers! Snickers and wise grins greeted me as I shamefacedly entered the right coach. More scenery to watch and more farewell notes; then, finally, the brakeman called: "Iron Mountain, next stop!"

Was I thrilled or just plain scared? I do not know, but my knees had a strange shakiness as I went down from the train and looked around the little town where Carmel is. That is when I wired you, because I knew you would be worried until you heard of my safe arrival. I took a taxi and was outside of the Carmel[5] in just a few minutes.

My heart was pounding so loudly that I thought the taxi driver would surely hear it. "Just call me, Miss, when you're ready to go," he said. "Oh, I won't be going anywhere," I stammered. "You mean you're gonna stay here?" "Yes," I gulped, "I am going to stay!" "Well, whatta ya know! So long, Miss, good luck and say some prayers for me too!" A friendly wave; the taxi was gone; and I stood alone outside the Carmel.

---

[5] "The Carmel" is another way of referring to "the Carmelite Monastery."

Letter writing time is over, so I shall tell you about my actually entering the cloister next time. Meanwhile, be sure to keep me in your prayers as I constantly keep you in mine. Jesus love you! Mary protect you!

Your loving daughter,
Marie

Letter Two

*D*earest Mother, Dad, and all,
Your letter was such a torrent of questions that our Mother thinks another letter from me will help to ease your minds. Writing to you will also help the loneliness I feel right now. Mother assured me that you at home as well as I will someday find a real joy in the sacrifice that this separation brings; but right now—well, it is better to talk of lighter things.

I think the last letter left me standing rather uneasily outside the monastery. It took me some time to muster enough courage to ring the doorbell. Then the extern sister graciously welcomed me with a smile that eased my bewildered mind.

"I am Marie ..."

"Oh, yes," Sister warmly replied before I could even say the last name, "you are our new little sister. Come right in. You can make a visit in the chapel while I call our Reverend Mother."

Mother and Dad, I could never describe my feelings as I went into the lovely little chapel. What peace is there! I was too excited to pray. I guess we do not have to pray with words at times like that. God understands and helps us even if we cannot stammer out our needs. I did remember one thing, though, and that was to beg Jesus and His sweet Mother, Mary, to bless all my loved ones.

Sister was soon back to take me to the parlor. That was an experience! You will have it sometime, so I had better prepare you. The little visiting room has several chairs and a table in it. There is a big grating on the one side, with a black curtain behind it. Somehow the reality is shocking even if you have read about it in books.

Finally, the curtain was drawn, and there stood the sweetest nun. The smile, the soft voice chased away most of my fear. As

Mother asked a few questions about the trip, I began to feel more at ease. Then Mother gave me a little explanation of life in Carmel: the routine, the little trials, and the joys that I might expect. When Mother asked if there were any questions I wished to ask, I just went blank. All that list of questions that we had put to each other before my departure left my mind; so I simply said there were none. A bell summoned the extern sister. "Sister will help you dress so that you can enter immediately," Mother said as Sister entered the room. Sister gave me the long black dress and left me, telling me to open the door as soon as I had dressed. Then Sister helped me arrange the little black postulant veil and the elbow-length black cape.

As soon as I had the postulant's outfit on, Sister took me back to the chapel—this time, right up to the Communion railing. After I had knelt, Sister gave me a lighted candle to hold. Then I noticed for the first time a big grate beside the sanctuary. The curtain on one side was drawn, and I could see sisters inside—but was I scared when I saw their faces veiled![6] "I wonder if that is the way they always are! Will I never see their faces? Dear Jesus, if that is Carmel and that is where you want me, give me the courage I need," I prayed, not daring to look again.

My reverie stopped when the sisters began to sing. I still keep hearing some of the words:

> Come, my daughter, come away
> Leave the world with all its dross,
> I would have thee watch and pray,
> I would have thee bear the cross!

---

[6] The veil is no longer lowered to cover the face. The grate itself is a sign of our separation from the world and our consecration to God. This grate is normally covered by a curtain.

Inside the Cloistered Life

Their voices sounded just like angels! Soon, too soon, they stopped, and Sister said we were going to the enclosure. When we reached the big door, I knocked three times, and then the door opened. "Kneel and kiss the Crucifix," a kind voice whispered. I did. The door shut and then the joy almost overpowered me as I realized, "I am in Carmel."

The sisters formed a procession and, chanting a hymn, entered the inside chapel. There, as I knelt right in the front, the sisters sang another beautiful hymn, after which we left the chapel. Guess what! All the sisters then raised their veils and welcomed me to Carmel.

We went through the monastery—but I am too mixed up to remember everything. As soon as I am more acquainted, I shall write to describe the different parts of our monastery so that you can picture them even more clearly than the album of pictures showed them. Please write to tell me how each one is. It is so good to hear from those at home. Oh, and be sure to keep praying for me as I am for you.

Your loving daughter,
Marie

Letter Three

*D*ear Mother and Dad and all,
      Praised be Jesus Christ!

This is how we greet each other whenever we meet. The sister thus greeted responds, "Now and forever" — and we both gain the indulgence attached to this beautiful aspiration. I still stumble over the response, but surely our dear Lord understands.

Just two weeks old in Carmel! Our Mother Prioress wants me to write to let you know that everything is going just fine. The daily routine and the many, many new things to learn are good helps for anyone who might have a case of homesickness. Your letters were so encouraging, Mother and Dad, and so very interesting. Please write often.

The first few weeks in Carmel our Reverend Mother does not permit the postulants to rise with the Community nor to go to Matins, which are said at 9:00 p.m.;[7] so, although the other sisters

---

[7] At present Matins are at 9:25 p.m. According to the Church's document on the Liturgy, the various Hours of the Divine Office should be at their proper time of day. See the appendix for the daily schedule now observed.

do rise at this time of the year at 5:30 a.m., I am still resting on my "hard" bed till 6:30 a.m. I must tell you my first experience on a Carmelite bed. It is just a big plank laid on two trestles, no head or foot save that the pillow is at one end and the blankets tucked in at the other end. The bed is quite narrow in comparison with our beds, and I really feared to turn over in the night without getting out of bed each time to do so. There was such a "squeak" each time that I feared it would wake the others. It was the board, Mother, not my bones!

The other day, I begged Reverend Mother to let me try getting up early with the other sisters. Her Reverence replied, "Well, your Charity can try it for a while, but I am sure you will soon appreciate the alleviations allowed newcomers." Our Mother and the sisters always say "your Charity" instead of "you" when addressing another sister.

As soon as the signal for rising sounds, each sister rises promptly. There is a real reason for so doing, even if it does seem to be the middle of the night. Each one tries to be the first to greet our dearest Lord with the prescribed Carmelite ritual. It took me several days before I could dust the sleep out of my eyes and shake off the drowsiness in order to follow the others. It has not happened yet; but maybe someday I really will be *first*!

You are probably wondering just what it is we strive to do first. I am sorry for not explaining sooner. You see, we have a little wooden object called "clappers" that consists of a stationary piece of flat wood about two by four inches in dimension to which are attached two loose pieces of wood, one on each side. By holding the handle and moving one's wrist rhythmically back and forth, one can make the loose boards clap against the stationary one.

That is just what we do first thing in the morning. We clap the boards—one, two, three, as evenly as possible; then again—one, two, three, in the same way; and finally a third time—one, two, three (something like the altar boys do at Mass on Holy Thursday when clappers replace the bells). We were taught to sound the three sets of three to honor the Most Blessed Trinity. As soon as we have finished sounding the clappers, we say: "Praised be Jesus Christ and the Virgin Mary, His Mother, come to prayer, sisters, come to praise the Lord!" And then we kiss the floor as an act of humility. Thus begins our Carmelite day.

Time to go, now, so I shall close, begging God's special blessing and Mary's loving protection for my beloved dad, mother, brothers, and sisters.

Your loving daughter,
Marie

Letter Four

*D*earest Mother, Dad, and all my dear ones,

Pax Christi! This is a heading with which Carmelites often start their letters. How fitting it is! Peace, Christ's peace emanates from the cloister to fill weary souls—to encourage struggling souls. We live in an atmosphere of peace and strive, by our prayers, to make others feel the same.

Carmelites certainly waste no time on the vanities of dress. I do not know how the sisters do it, but everyone is dressed and ready for morning prayers in just a few minutes. Maybe the cold water has something to do with it. We each have a basin[8] that we fill the night before for use in the morning. The water is so cold that it certainly puts life and a wide-awake feeling in me. This is one mortification that is really hard—but if the others can save souls by so doing, I shall offer it up for that all-important intention too.

The clappers mentioned in a previous letter have another use: If sounded quickly like a rattle, it is a signal for the novices to go to the Novitiate. When I am about half finished dressing, the clappers sound for morning prayers, and all the sisters except your

---

[8] In our present monastery, each sister has a sink in her cell.

"slow-poke" go immediately to the Novitiate. At least the past two mornings, I have been one prayer earlier than before—but I am still late. Please pray that I become quicker.

What an embarrassing moment I had the other day! The postulant veil is black with a white handkerchief inside (this white folds back about an inch over the black veil right in front). Well, in my rush to be on time for prayers, I quickly put on the veil and tied the tapes. On entering the Novitiate and kneeling in my place, which is way up front, I heard some snickers behind me. "What have I done now?" was my first thought. The enlightenment was soon to come. Our Mother was beside me, removing the veil; then her Reverence gently turned it right side out and made a sign to me to retie the tapes. It must have been quite a sight to see the white drapery dangling down the back of my head! We laughed heartily at recreation about the new headdress. The sisters were sorry that they snickered during prayers, but it is really a hard thing to control oneself perfectly at all times.

As soon as morning prayers are finished, we (the novices) go in procession down to the Choir, reciting the *Miserere*.[9] I do not recite yet, because it is all I can do to watch the Latin words out of a corner of my eye as I look out for the stairs, landing, and turns on the way down, but I am anxious to get well enough acquainted in order to join the sisters in this act of reparation for the sins of the world.

We join the professed sisters in the Choir, where, after reciting the Angelus, we make our hour of mental prayer and then recite

[9] Psalm 51 in modern translations, or Psalm 50 in the Vulgate and Douay-Rheims. "Have mercy on me, O God, according to thy great mercy." These psalms, still called by the first word in Latin, are now recited in English.

the Divine Office. Holy Mass, followed by the precious time of "thanksgiving" after Communion, completes our morning prayer.

After the meager breakfast (we are in the season of monastic fast), the novices have an hour's instruction period. Then we are sent to help the professed sisters with the various offices (works) of the monastery. At about seven minutes to eleven, we are summoned to the Choir to make the particular examen of conscience. This is followed by dinner and the noon recreation, after which we return to Choir for the daily visit to the Blessed Sacrament. This visit is "in common," but throughout the day we may snatch free moments to make short visits to our dear Lord. How joyous are these moments: near to Him in our little Choir, whose stark simplicity has a peace all its own. You must hear about the Choir in detail; but now I want to complete the daily schedule for you.

The visit is followed by an hour of strict silence during which we pray, read, write, or work quietly. The sisters told me that I will appreciate the permission given in the holy *Rule* to spend this hour resting during the summer months when we rise very early. Then at two o'clock we recite Vespers, say the Litany of our Blessed Mother, and spend the remaining time until three o'clock reading some spiritual book.

Again, after the spiritual reading period ends, we go to our work, whatever that may be, until the clappers sound at a quarter to five in the evening. This is the signal to prepare for mental prayer or meditation, which lasts from five o'clock until six o'clock. This hour fortifies and nourishes our souls; then we take the bodily food at the six o'clock collation (or supper).

Another hour of wholesome recreation has us ready to resume the life of prayer with Compline at eight o'clock, which is followed by the "Asperges" or the sprinkling with holy water—the exterior sign of the cleansing away of all the little faults committed that day for which we have repented. Then follow the evening prayers to our Blessed Mother, our father St. Joseph, and the saints of our holy Order, begging protection for the night. After this, we have free time to spend in prayer until nine o'clock, when we recite Matins and Lauds of the Divine Office. Our day closes with the examination of conscience, after which we retire between ten thirty and eleven o'clock.

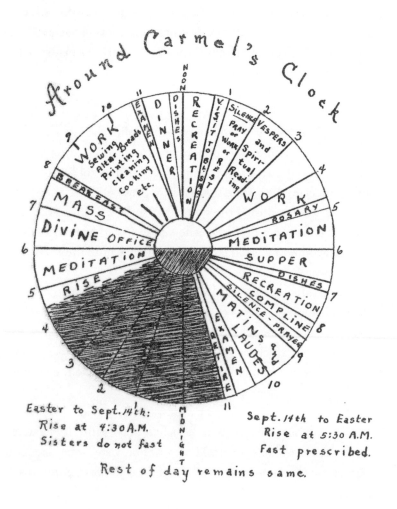

Around Carmel's Clock

Easter to Sept. 14th:
Rise at 4:30 A.M.
Sisters do not fast

Sept. 14th to Easter
Rise at 5:30 A.M.
Fast prescribed.

Rest of day remains same.

Now you will know just what I am doing throughout the day, and you can unite yourself with us as we spend the precious hours in prayer. You share in all my prayers in a very special way.

Your loving daughter,
Marie

Letter Five

*D*earest Mother, Dad, and all,
 May Christ's peace fill your souls! Do you remember
the details of my learning to drive: how my "big" brother offered
to teach me when he was out with the delivery truck? I shall never
forget the afternoon that I mistook the gas pedal for the brake and,
instead of slowing down on the curve behind the rectory, went
head-on into Father's wooden fence. No one, especially that dear
brother of mine, ever allowed me to forget that!

Well, now there are some more similar (if not quite as exciting)
incidents to add to that one. You are probably wondering what
could cause such happenings behind our cloister wall. I shall hasten
to satisfy that curiosity.

Actually, the cause of the commotion is the most wonderful
part of our contemplative life—the duty of reciting the Divine
Office in Choir. When our Mother began to explain the Divine
Office to me, her Reverence quoted a passage that so struck me
that I asked to copy it. It was in the work of Abbot Marmion and
it ran as follows: "The Divine Office ... is an infinitely pleasing
homage of praise to God, which together with the Mass, around
which it gravitates, forms the most complete expression of religion."

I tried to pay close attention to all the explanations; but, as with the driving, there have been so many mistakes. The breviary (or Office book) has so many strings, and I always pulled the wrong one. Everything seemed rather clear during the explanation; but once we began to recite the Office in Choir, your Carmelite was so completely lost that she almost became discouraged. Our Mother amazed me! Her Reverence could keep finding my place while at the same time she kept reciting with the others.

Yet not withstanding all the trials associated with the Divine Office, it gives me real joy to be allowed to take part in this, the great prayer of Holy Mother Church. Priests and nuns are deputed to offer this tribute to God as ambassadors for the whole Mystical Body—and wonderful to say, your child has a place in this group. You are probably wondering just what the Divine Office is.

The Office is made up primarily of the Psalms, those beautiful hymns of praise, petition, thanksgiving, and love that the holy king David composed and that our good Jesus and His holy Mother repeated in the Jewish synagogues of old. To the Psalms are added passages from both the Old and New Testaments and prayers in which the Church gathers up the intentions of all her children that she might make supplication for their needs. The Office, following the liturgical cycle, brings before us each day some mystery of Our Lord's life, some feast of Our Blessed Mother, or a saint.

It is divided into seven parts or hours. Matins and Lauds, which we recite at nine o'clock in the evening, form the night office.[10] To the hymn and Psalms are added lessons that are an instruction from Scripture, a brief résumé of the mystery or the life of the saint, and a commentary on the Gospel of the day's Mass. These are followed by that most magnificent of all hymns

---

[10] Lauds is now prayed at its proper time in the morning.

of praise—the *Te Deum*. Lauds, as the name implies, is an act of loving praise.

In the morning we say Prime, Terce, Sext, and None.[11] The prayers of Prime are so well suited to begin the day, directing our every thought and act to the glory of God and calling on Jesus, His Immaculate Mother, and the saints for all the help needed to accomplish God's will.

We say Vespers at two o'clock each afternoon. How we love to unite with Mary in her hymn, the *Magnificat*. Our fervent desire is that this loving Mother pray in us and adore her Son, our God. With Compline, at eight o'clock each evening, we have the Church's night prayer, the closing of the Divine Office for that day. We thank God for all His blessings both to ourselves and to the whole world; beg His protection for the night; and close with a lovely tribute to Mary, singing the *Salve Regina*.

Now that you know how wonderful a privilege has been given your daughter, you should hear how her initial efforts turned out. As I told you, I thought that my whole attention was given when things were explained—but I had some rude awakenings. Besides the intricacies of the breviary with all its strings and completely Latin text (including the directions), there are so many regulations about standing, sitting, and turning in Choir.

Imagine the confusion when, one day, I followed the sister who stands beside me out to the center of the Choir. Sister had a duty to perform as part of the ceremonial of the Office. But I—well, I just stood there, wondering what to do next, until another sister came and gently pulled me back to the side!

---

[11] Prime has been suppressed in the Divine Office. Terce, Sext, and None are now prayed as near as possible to their proper times, as indicated by the very names: third, sixth, and ninth hours.

Another time, turning the wrong way had me face-to-face with the sister next to me. Poor Sister could not help snickering. The worst happened during a solemnly chanted Office. The chantress had chanted the initial part of the Gospel, after which there was a pause. All the others sat down so that Sister could continue her

lesson. But I, standing right up front, thought something should be said—so, during the prescribed pause, I filled in with a very solemn "Deo gratias!" That is one Gregorian response that is easy to remember.[12]

But gradually, the rough edges are becoming smoother. Now I can follow along with the recitation, and I can usually find the place. This, the most powerful prayer there is, includes the needs of each one of my loved ones, as well as priests and those who recommend themselves to our prayers.

I like to think of the Office as "an atom bomb of grace" that we can throw out into the world to secure its return to Christ. You can pray with us by uniting all you do with our Divine Office.

Your loving daughter,
"Sister" Marie

---

[12] Certain hours of the Divine Office are sung with Gregorian chant: Lauds and Vespers on all solemnities and some feasts. On bigger solemnities Matins is chanted. Vespers is chanted every Sunday.

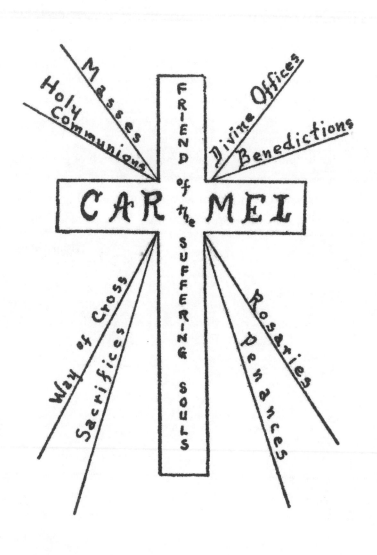

Letter Six

*D*ear Mother, Dad, and all my loved ones,
Praised be Jesus Christ!

You will rejoice when you hear how often we remember our dear dead here in Carmel, not only during the month of November but every day of every month. Surely the souls recommended to our prayers, the souls of our own relatives and friends, as well as all the suffering souls benefit from our Carmelite life.

Each day, as you know, the dead are remembered at the Holy Sacrifice of the Mass. It is the same at the Divine Office, each part of which includes a memento of the faithful departed. On one afternoon, each week, we say Vespers of the Dead for all our relatives, friends, and benefactors. Three times during the year, a period of several weeks is set aside, during which period we recite the Office of the Dead three times and chant three requiem high Masses. Of course, on All Souls' Day we say the complete Office and join with Holy Mother Church in her suffrages for the dead.

All Souls' Day brought me a real shock! I had been told when the Office of the Dead would begin and how it differed somewhat from other Offices, but I had not been forewarned about the *catafalque*.[13] What a shock it was to enter the Choir and find a coffin covered with a black pall and surrounded by the six funeral candles. "I wonder who died!" I gasped. "They must have forgotten to tell me in the confusion." I struggled not to cry, thinking, "Whoever it is, she is my sister." After the Office, no one else looked disturbed. That puzzled me. Finally, I asked our Mother. I was surely relieved when her Reverence took me back to Choir, lifted the pall, and exposed only the wooden *catafalque*. How the sisters laughed that night when they heard of the postulant's consternation!

The privilege of gaining the plenary indulgence at each visit to the church is ours not only on November 2 but also on July 16, the feast of Our Lady of Mount Carmel. We try to make as many visits these days as we can.[14] You know, anyone who visits a Carmelite church on July 16 can gain the same indulgence for each visit by simply saying the prescribed prayers. Again, on August 2, we have, by special privilege, the opportunity of gaining the Portiuncula indulgence for every visit to our own chapel. How generous Holy Mother Church is to allow us these many occasions on which we can help the suffering souls!

Besides these extraordinary helps, we have daily practices that must bring much relief to the dead. As we go to the refectory for dinner and for supper (or collation), we recite the *De Profundis*,[15] a psalm that well sums up the sighs and pleadings of the holy souls. At the end of this psalm, we recite the prayer for all the faithful departed. While we are washing the dishes after dinner and supper,

---

[13] In the new rubrics, the *catafalque* is no longer used.

[14] According to current norms in the Church, only one plenary indulgence may be gained in a day.

[15] Psalm 130 in modern translations, Psalm 129 in the Vulgate and Douay-Rheims. "Out of the depths I have cried to thee, O Lord: Lord, hear my voice."

we say aloud many prayers for the dead. Is it not beautiful that every moment of our Carmelite day is an act of love for God, a source of good for souls? The daily recitation of the Rosary, making the Way of the Cross, and striving to make many spiritual communions throughout the day are other means that we employ to help our loved dead.

A beautiful custom brings us to our knees each evening (at eight o'clock in the winter, and nine o'clock in summer). The monastery bells are tolled, during which time everyone stops whatever she is doing to kneel and recite the *De Profundis*. Again, the prayer for all the faithful departed completes the psalm. As the last "may they rest in peace" fades away, we have an inner assurance that many souls have benefited from our prayers that day, and our hearts are filled with the hope that one more saint is glorifying God in Heaven because our prayers have hastened his deliverance from Purgatory.

You, too, Dad and Mother, can join your little Carmelite in these prayers. Often make ejaculations and to try to say the Rosary every day. You will find a great joy in the thought that you are really helping your own loved dead as well as all the suffering souls.

May Jesus bless you and Mary guard you—this is my daily prayer for all of you.

Your loving daughter,
"Sister" Marie

Letter Seven

*D*ear Mother, Dad, and all my loved ones,
   Come, O come Emmanuel!

Gaudete Sunday is set aside for writing a Christmas letter home. May you have the choicest blessings this Christmas, the peace, the joy that Christ came to give. We shall be together, although more than a thousand miles is between us; for at the Mass, we are truly in the stable, and as we visit our dear Lord in His tabernacle, we shall be kneeling together at His manger. How wonderful these things are!

Advent in Carmel—this is a thrilling experience. Neither the glitter of pre-Christmas decorations nor the excitement of gift-shopping tours nor the many preparations that filled my days before Christmas in years gone by ever gave me the genuine happiness that our days of preparation in Carmel have given me this year. How I wish you could share these joys!

The first Sunday of Advent, New Year's Day in the Church year, was a day of recollection or retreat for the whole community. Extra hours of prayer and reading, together with the silence observed on such a day, helped me think much about the only worthwhile things: God; His infinite love for each soul; and the way we can repay that love. We drew very close to our Immaculate Mother, placing all our Advent exercises in her hands so that she would help us to prepare well for the birth of Jesus.

Then began a lovely custom. Each day during Advent, one sister makes a private retreat. We have a beautiful statue of the Infant Jesus lying in the manger. On her private retreat day, each sister may keep this statue in her cell as an added incentive to meditate on the mystery of Christmas. The private retreat ends after supper; so when Sister comes to the evening recreation, she brings this lovely statue of the Infant Jesus with her. At the end of recreation, the sister whose retreat will be the next day goes up to her cell. The other sisters, being assembled in the recreation room, go singing an Advent hymn while taking the Infant Jesus in procession to Sister's cell.

How we long for our day of retreat! It is truly wonderful to think about what Christmas really means. On that day, we do not have to work in any of the offices of the monastery; but we spend our time in our cell working during the hours not set aside for reading or prayer. Those who have the holy Habit wear a special veil in retreat. This is lowered over the face when the sister walks through the monastery.[16] I was wondering how I could pull our little veil over my face; but our Mother said that postulants cannot do that. So I had to seclude myself by guarding against looking at things that could distract me. I did pray much for you and for all in the world, begging the good God that all might realize just a little bit the wondrous love that Christ's birth means; the peace, the joy it brings.

We are making a mystic manger in which to receive our newborn King. The Christmas novena, which is entirely different from anything you ever heard, will be our manger. Each day, we meditate on some phase in the journey of Mary and Joseph to Bethlehem, sing special hymns, and recite particular prayers that commemorate their sufferings at being refused a lodging and having to find shelter in a stable. Our many acts of love each day will make a little pillow on which the Divine Babe can rest His little head. Little acts of mortification such as walking quietly down the stairs, conquering our curiosity, and answering the bell immediately are the straws with which we will fill the manger. Prayers to our Blessed Mother make the swaddling bands to cover her Divine Babe.

Advent means another penance too—double work; but we love that as a means of journeying with Mary and Joseph over the rough, hard way to Bethlehem. The sister-printers are very busy

---

[16] With the current norms for papal enclosure, the veil is no longer lowered over the face.

finishing the Christmas card orders.[17] I helped with the printing and, as usual, had some mishaps. Smudges of ink and crooked designs were the results of my first attempts. Since the paper is expensive, it was against holy poverty to waste the cards; so each of us offered to send our soiled cards to family and friends. Now, my stack is so high that I shall have to acquire many, many friends or else store the cards away for future Christmas seasons.

This explains your rather smudgy card; but however it looks, it brings my love's best wishes. More than that, it is the bearer of the promise that we shall meet at the manger to wish our dear Savior a "happy birthday" and to receive His wonderful gifts.

Your loving daughter,
"Sister" Marie

---

[17] The Iron Mountain Carmel no longer takes orders for printing as it is not very compatible with our life of prayer.

Letter Eight

ear Mother, Dad, and all,

May Christ's gift to each of you this Christmas season be His own sweet peace to last throughout the coming year!

Were you thinking of your Carmelite on Christmas Eve and Christmas Day as she was thinking of you? I could imagine how rushed Dad was during the weeks preceding the great feast, and I prayed that he would be able to manage all the work. I was with Mother "in spirit" as she and Sis arranged the manger and the Christmas decorations in the living room, and I was wondering how my "big" brother managed the outdoor decorations without his usual companion.

We were busy, too, and that activity kept me from feeling too homesick. Do you want to hear how we spent Christmas Eve and Christmas? Before describing that, however, I do want to thank you for the lovely gifts. The flowers that Dad sent are on the high altar right near our dear Infant Savior. They keep reminding the sacramental Jesus that you love Him and how they plead for graces for you. What a delightful surprise it was when the new steam iron came up out of the beautifully wrapped box. Mother, you have the grateful prayers of all the sisters for that practical gift.

Salted nuts from my dear brother prove that he still remembers his sister's favorites, and the box of lovely materials and decorations for making Infant Jesus of Prague outfits is a sign that Sis knows more about Carmel than I thought she did. May God reward and bless you, each one of you, in the way only He can for making my Christmas so happy!

As you read this little description of our Christmas, just keep remembering that you had *the* special place in all the beautiful prayers we said. There is really so much to tell you that it will be very hard to include it in one letter, but I shall try.

We began the joyous festival early on Christmas Eve morning. At Prime (the part of the Divine Office that is said first every day) we always read the Martyrology. This gives a brief account of the saints whose feast will be the next day. Christmas Eve, therefore, was the morning on which Christ's birth was announced.

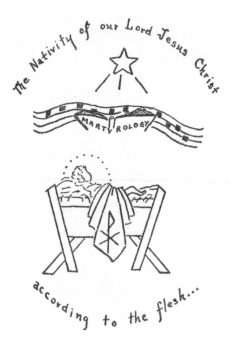

How solemn is the ceremony that tells of this blessed birth. We chanted Prime that morning instead of simply reciting it. All the sisters wore the white mantle. At the time of the Martyrology, our Reverend Mother, accompanied by two lay-sisters, each of whom carried a lighted candle, brought the book to the lectern in the center of the Choir. Then, her Reverence chanted the announcement in the thrilling, majestic Gregorian melody. After the other parts of the Divine Office and Holy Mass, I had a really pleasant surprise. Our Mother wished each of us a joyous Christmas, and then we wished each other the same. In my heart, I told Jesus and Mary to wish you the same, for I knew I could be the first to say it to you that way.[18]

The rest of Christmas Eve was spent arranging the mangers in the Choir, in the Novitiate, and in the community room. Vespers at two o'clock were solemnly chanted.[19] After supper, our Mother gave us the mail and gifts we had received. Your beautiful and useful gifts made my Christmas even happier. We had a delightful time seeing each other's surprises and sharing each other's joy. We could have gone to rest, but we were too excited to feel tired. This is the *one* only night in the whole year when there is no strict silence; so we sang hymns all evening until it was time for our procession with the Infant Jesus: meditation and Compline were earlier than usual that day. I could imagine your last-minute rush to have all the gifts wrapped, and how busy you and Sis were stuffing turkey and preparing the festal breakfast for after Midnight Mass.

---

[18] The ceremony described here is now placed before First Vespers of Christmas. Two novices usually hold the candles as there are no longer lay-sisters.

[19] Vespers is prayed at its proper time in the evening.

At about fifteen minutes to ten, we assembled in the Novitiate. All the sisters had on the white mantle, and each of us carried a lighted candle. We began to sing the lovely hymn "Jesu Dulcis Memoria" and then started in procession through the monastery. Our Reverend Mother walked last carrying a most beautiful life-size statue of the Infant Jesus. Having entered the Choir, we knelt at our places. Then our Mother presented the Infant Jesus to each one of us that we might kiss Him.

It was a little after ten o'clock when we began the Divine Office of Christmas. We chanted all of Matins. Oh, how joyous was the Gregorian chant for this holy night! The *Te Deum* of Matins was just completed in time for the solemn Midnight Mass. I was right beside you (in spirit) as we adored the Divine Babe when Father raised the consecrated Host. Immediately after Mass—about 1:00 a.m., or a little after—we began Lauds.[20] Again, the Gregorian chant was thrilling. We left the Choir about a quarter to two (a.m.), had breakfast, and wished each other all the joys of the holy day. After breakfast, some of the sisters went to rest, but most of the younger ones returned to the Choir to stay with the Divine Babe.

Christmas morning we were awakened not by an alarm or clappers but by the sisters who sang hymns. As we finished dressing, we joined them until the bell for prayer. Mental prayer and the Divine Office were followed by two Masses. I read all your most welcome letters after the Masses. How close you seemed in spite of the distance between us.

Stuffed fish took the place of turkey, but kind benefactors made sure that we had all the trimmings. The candy you sent was a very tasty treat. May God reward and bless each of you for making my

[20] As said above, Lauds is prayed in the morning.

Christmas in Carmel possible and for increasing its joy with your gifts.

How beautiful the chanted Vespers were on that day of days! You were with me again in spirit when at Benediction in the afternoon we adored our newborn Savior. It is a holy custom in Carmel to spend half of evening meditation on Christmas and the three following days singing carols to our Infant King.[21] It reminded me of the happy evenings we spent singing carols at the manger at home. I hope you did the same this year as we did other years.

You are in my daily prayers to the Babe who holds us in His tiny hands. May Mary keep you ever close to Jesus.

Your loving daughter,
"Sister" Marie

---

[21] The nuns now observe the full hour of mental prayer. There are, however, plenty of opportunities for singing carols!

Letter Nine

*D*ear Mother, Dad, and all my loved ones,

Come, let us adore our newborn King!

There have been so many wonderful surprises during these past few weeks. Christmas is not just a day in Carmel, it is a whole season. Even the monastic fast observed during this part of the year is dispensed on Christmas and the three following days.

December twenty-eighth, the feast of the Holy Innocents, found some of us the willing victims of tricks. A very tall sister found her mantle was knee length at Vesper-time while the shortest one in the house had a trailing mantle. During recreation, we received a lovely dish of fruit, on top of which was a banana. Sister started to cut the banana in order to share it, but it seemed that a saw would be required to cut through it. (Investigation proved that the center was a wad of cotton, not fruit.)

My "big" brother had very special prayers on New Year's Eve. I hope everyone made his twenty-first birthday a very happy occasion. Our permission to stay up in prayer until midnight gave opportunities of saying many extra prayers for him, prayers that begged Jesus' and Mary's special blessing on his life.

We, the novices, entertained the senior sisters on the feast of the Sweet Name of Jesus. We made up some songs and verses to sing and recite. The menu was a combination of all our favorite dishes made with what was at hand, even if some required ingredients were missing. In the evening, we had a play about the Nativity. All the old pieces of silk we could gather were arranged into the royal robes of the Magi. My face was charcoaled so that the Ethiopian king would be represented. The shepherds had various kinds of cloth draped like pictures we saw on Christmas cards. For lighting effects, we salvaged all the colored cellophane that came on gifts. This red cellophane plus a small light and several branches of Christmas trees made a realistic fire for the shepherds.

Everything was going rather well until the part where the star appeared. "Look at that beautiful star," the one king said as he pointed where we had taped a large star. Just at that moment, the tape loosened, and down went the star! Then, when the angels appeared (standing on covered boxes), someone stepped on the hem of a makeshift gown, and down went the angel, wings and all! But we covered over these mishaps by inserting some extra hymns. Everyone agreed that, all in all, the play was good. We had a wonderful time doing it.

The biggest surprise came on the feast of the Epiphany. That Office is so beautiful, filled as it is with love and adoration. At evening prayer time, all the sisters put on their white mantles and assembled in the Choir. Our Mother gave a beautiful talk on the meaning of the vows and how comparable they are to the three gifts of the Magi: the gold of our *obedience*, which is the offering of our most precious treasure, our will; the frankincense of *poverty*, which makes our complete trust in God alone arise as sweet perfume to His throne; and the mysterious myrrh, our vow of *chastity*, which sublimates the natural instincts into Divine Love, thus making us die to all that is purely human. This is but one of the many mystic significations given to the gifts that the three kings brought to Bethlehem.

Then, beginning with our Mother, each sister took her turn to renew her vows. I was allowed to propose to observe the virtues of poverty, chastity, and obedience until such time as God wills for me to make vows.[22]

You may wonder about the reason for a renovation of vows. The final professed sister makes solemn vows, which are binding until death; but to inspire a new vigor and fervor, the custom is observed of renewing the vows publicly twice a year. There is something so inspiring about this practice. It makes me earnestly desire to have

---

[22] The solemn renewal of vows is now observed on the solemnity of the Holy Cross, September 14. There is a simpler renewal on February 2, the World Day of Consecrated Life.

that total consecration that the vows give. Pray with me that I may be found worthy to make profession when the time comes.

Time to go now; may our dear Lord and His wonderful Mother, Mary, love, bless, and protect each one of you during this New Year!

Your loving daughter,
"Sister" Marie

Letter Ten

*D*ear Mother, Dad, and all,
    Praised be Jesus Christ!

This is a good season in which to tell you something about Carmel's devotion to the Infant Jesus. From the holy cards I sent home, you know that our Blessed Lady of Mount Carmel is represented holding her Divine Babe; hence, it is but natural that we, her children, should show special marks of love for her firstborn Son.

In the Novitiate oratory, there is a most beautiful life-size statue of the Infant Jesus. From our first day in Carmel, this Child is set before us as the model on which we mold our lives. I think you would like to know what we strive to imitate in the Child Jesus; you could, even in your own everyday life, try to practice the same virtues. It is all summed up in this set of maxims:

> Learn of the Infant Jesus to be little and to believe without
> doubt, to obey without reluctance, to be in want without
> murmuring, to work without presumption, to live in a spirit
> of humility and simplicity, and to strive for nothing else
> than to please God.

I did not know, before my entering Carmel, that so many Carmelite saints had special devotion to the Infant Jesus or the Child Jesus. In my rather crooked way of looking at things, I thought that the austerity of Carmel would take one's gaze from the lovely Infant and focus it exclusively on the Man of Sorrows! How wrong that idea was, I soon discovered.

It is quite commonly known that our little Carmelite saint of modern times, St. Thérèse of Lisieux, had great devotion to the Child Jesus. She taught the way of childlike abandonment to the Divine Will, for she wished to be the plaything of the Divine Child so that He could do with her as He pleased.

But St. Thérèse is only one in a long line of Carmelite saints who have practiced devotion to the Child Jesus. The great mystic and reformer of Carmel, St. Teresa of Jesus,[23] was once aware of the presence of a lovely little boy. He came near to her and spoke:

"What is your name?"

"I am called Teresa of Jesus. And what is your name?"

He smiled and joyfully answered: "I am Jesus of Teresa."

Others, too, such as St. Albert of Sicily, who held the Divine Babe in his arms, and the Ven. Sister Marguerite of Beaune, France, who often saw and spoke with the Infant Jesus, are examples of Carmel's devotedness to the Infant Jesus.

The most amazing discovery I made in this regard was that the now widespread devotion to the Infant Jesus of Prague had its origin in Carmel. I know you are looking very dubious about that statement—as did I the day it was mentioned.

---

[23] More commonly known as St. Teresa of Ávila. It was St. John Paul II, a great devotee of Carmel, who requested that she be referred to with her religious title: St. Teresa of Jesus.

Our Mother, one day, sent me to help the sister who makes outfits for the Infant Jesus of Prague statues. As I sat there learning how to sew the beautifully adorned little dresses and mantles, there were many questions racing through my mind. Really, I had only seen one statue of the Infant of Prague before entering Carmel, and, as you know, that was under a glass dome at the cathedral.

"THE MORE YOU HONOR ME, THE MORE I WILL BLESS YOU."

"Who orders all these statues?" I wondered. "In what does the devotion consist? How and where did it start?" I could not doubt that it was approved, but I wondered why I had never been told about it. Well, when recreation began, the torrent of questions was let loose. Knowing that you will be as interested in hearing the answers as I was, I shall try to recall as much of the history as I can.

In the early seventeenth century, after the war had left the Carmelite monastery in Prague completely destitute,[24] the princess gave the friars her much-loved statue of the Infant Jesus that He might help them. Invasion shortly after caused the friars to flee from Prague in such haste that the loved statue was left behind. Some years later, when peace was restored, the Carmelites returned to their monastery. The precious statue of the Infant was found by Father Cyril in the rubbish. Since that time, countless miracles have been wrought through devotion to this miraculous statue.

The statues we dress go to churches and homes. How the Divine Child must love to reign in the parish or the family circle! This is no advertising campaign, Mother and Dad; but I do wish that you would purchase an Infant for the house. Maybe someday you will have the means to give a large one to our parish.

We have a perpetual novena through which we recommend daily all the needs of our benefactors, the intentions recommended to our prayers, and all those for whom we should pray to the gracious "little King." Please join with us in honoring this Divine Child, who promised Father Cyril: "The more you honor Me, the more I will bless you!"

It is time to go now, but I do want to leave you one beautiful thought about the Infant Jesus. Father Faber expressed everything when he said:

---

[24] Princess Polyxena Lobkowitz, wife of High Chancellor Zdeněk Vojtěch Popel of Lobkowitz, presented this statue to the Carmelite friars of Prague in 1628. This statue became known as the Infant of Prague and is visited by pilgrims to this day.

Art Thou, sweet Child, my very God?
   Ah, I must love Thee then;
Love Thee and yearn to spread Thy love
   Among forgetful men.

Let us stay close to Jesus and His sweet Mother at every moment of every day.

Your loving daughter,
"Sister" Marie

Letter Eleven

*D*earest Mother, Dad, and all my loved ones,
    Praised be Jesus Christ!

What is this notion you have concerning my "starving to death" in Carmel? It calls for some explanation so that your minds can be at peace.

The only fact that your informer really had correct was about our not eating meat. We *never* eat meat except in the case (permitted by the holy *Rule*) of one who is ill or convalescing—in which case the sister eats out of the refectory or apart from the others.

Our meals are simple but substantial. Right now we are *fasting*, which means we follow the most recent "rules for fasting" as given by our Very Reverend Father General in 1947. According to these, breakfast consists of three ounces (including a small cup of coffee and dry bread).[25] During Lent, on all other fast days of the Church, and on every Friday throughout the year (Paschal Time excepted), the coffee is black.

---

[25] The Church promulgated new rules for fasting. These are followed and the portions are no longer individually weighed.

Inside the Cloistered Life

At eleven o'clock in the morning, we have dinner—a good, hearty meal of vegetables, fish, bread, and fruit. On all Fridays of the year, except in Paschal Time, we have no milk foods (butter, cheese, etc.) and no eggs; but every other day of the week, these foods form a good part of the menu, thus making up to some extent for the lack of meat.

At six o'clock in the evening, we have our collation. During this time of fasting, it consists of about ten ounces of food: during Lent, only eight ounces are permitted.

From Easter until September 14—the time when there is no fast—breakfast and supper are real meals. Now, you see, Mother, I am far from "starving to death." It is really a marvelous thing that everything tastes so good, even the foods I would not touch at home. There are probably two reasons for this: the grace of the vocation and the great emptiness I feel at eleven o'clock each morning and at six o'clock in the evening.

As you may already know, religious do not call their place of eating a dining room; it is the *refectory*. Our refectory would interest you. It is a large rectangular room with tables along each of the side walls.

There is a head table at which our Reverend Mother Prioress and Mother Sub-Prioress sit. Behind this, that is on the front wall of the room, there is a large wooden cross with an inscription beneath each arm: "Go to the Cross as to the table"; "Go to the table as to the Cross." On the center of this head table is placed a human skull—a reminder of our last end and the shortness of life. Sometimes this skull frightens the new sisters, but it really did not affect me at all.

At the lower end of the refectory is the pulpit, where one of the sisters sits to read during dinner and supper or collation. The reading is varied, consisting of some portion of our holy *Rule*,

Constitutions, or *Ceremonial,* and then the life of a saint or some other spiritual book. Sometimes I am so interested in the reading that I forget to eat, but our Mother says that both can be done at the same time. I shall have to learn that art, for thus far, I have been eating during most of the time when I should be helping with the dishes. (No remarks from Sis that this is to be expected—or that I am just trying to escape an odious duty!)

That reminds me of one foolish thing I did in the refectory. After the noon examen, we enter the refectory two by two reciting the psalm *De Profundis*, and after making a profound inclination to the Cross, each one goes to her respective place. The younger sisters stand at the lower end of the refectory, while the seniors are up at the front end. My first week in Carmel found me, each time, standing up in Reverend Mother's place. Now, as I look back, I wonder why I was so stupid. I might have seen where my companions went. Reverend Mother only smiled each time, as she told me to go and stand beside my "angel" (the novice appointed to guide me during my first two weeks in Carmel).

It is so wonderful to know that even eating is a prayer, an act of obedience, and, because of certain privations, a mortification pleasing to our dear Lord. We never really thought about that angle at home. If Sis burns the toast, then everyone can offer up the mortification; and if Mother makes her best apple pie, then all of you can do as we do—thank God for the treat and offer that up too. Thinking of God and offering Him even such a necessary action makes one's life just that much more worthwhile.

I know you keep me in your prayers, and you know that you are in mine always. Let us start offering up all our actions to Jesus for the salvation of souls.

Your loving daughter,
"Sister" Marie

Letter Twelve

*D*earest Mother, Dad, and all,
Praised be Jesus Christ!

You will never guess what duty your daughter has this week! It surprised her as much as it pleased her. Maybe the net result will be that most of the sisters will be sick—but I am in the kitchen.

Every Saturday, toward the end of our noon meal, the reader stops reading the spiritual book just long enough to read out the "Board of Offices" for the next week. The different duties connected with the choral recitation of the Divine Office change each Saturday; so, too, many other duties such as ringing the bell, serving at table, reading during meals, and cooking.

Usually there are three lay-sisters who do most of the domestic work.[26] These sisters are called by Jesus to serve Him in this way, and although they enjoy all the privileges of the Order, they are not required to assist at the Divine Office. A specified number of *Paters* (Our Fathers) replaces the recitation of the Divine Office, thus leaving our dear lay-sisters free to do other work while the

---

[26] According to *Perfectae Caritatis* no. 15, the status of lay-sisters has been suppressed. All the nuns share the domestic work.

Choir nuns are at the Office. They have solemn vows, are strictly cloistered, and wear the same Habit as the Choir nuns.

The novices (and postulants) usually help in the kitchen. It is good for all the sisters to be acquainted with the work so that in case of emergency, anyone can supply. Our Mother also said such work makes us practice obedience and helps us acquire the virtue of humility. However, I do find the work a real source of joy. Just the thought that one is serving Christ's spouses—giving them the nourishment required to accomplish His will—is a motivation to work as hard as possible.

But now some concrete facts about being "Carmel's cook"! Our little lay-sister prepares the meager breakfast while we are saying the

morning Office. Spiritual reading and instruction for the novices follows breakfast: then we go to our special duties. Mother, you should make Sis wear an apron like the one we wear! It is a big coverall (smock-like), only very long, with a belt. The elbow-length sleeves hold back securely our wool sleeves so that no part of the holy Habit (or in my case, the postulant's dress) ever gets dirty.

We do not decide what we shall cook. No, obedience is the guide in this as in all else. An experienced sister has the provisory (the Carmelite name for the pantry where all the food is kept). She makes the menu, which is given to our Mother for approval. Then she gives all the needed foods and recipes to the cook, who follows her directions and who should do everything just as the Provisor tells her, even if she has some "pet notion" as to how the thing can best be done. The Provisor has a big job: watching all the food so that nothing is wasted; weighing out the exact amounts so that we keep our fast; and seeing to it that the food is well prepared.

Thus far the cooking has not been too different from what we did at home, but I have learned several new ways of preparing fish, since we do not eat meat. Peeling enough vegetables is the biggest problem. I am still quite slow and have to have much help; but all the novices are sympathetic, having had the same difficulties. We "peel" at recreation until everything is done. Toasting enough bread for the community is a lengthy process, and, of course, there were many cinder-like pieces the first time I did it—but the sisters do not seem to mind eating extra-dark toast.

I really blundered twice already. One day, when the Provisor was gone, I needed an onion. There was just one funny-looking onion left in the bag—so, although it looked strange, I used it. What a look of consternation came over Sister when on her return I made a sign about the funny onion. Later I found out it was garlic. Another day I was figuring out some measurements for a large amount. Without my noticing it, the eraser slipped off our pencil and fell into the bowl next to me! Sister was surely surprised when she started to chew it at the noon meal. How we laughed when, at recreation, Sister remarked about the "chewy meal"!

But in spite of the difficulties, it is a very pleasant duty. The quiet peace of our large, bright kitchen makes one think of God. I like to work with our Blessed Mother, asking her to let me do all just as she did it in the little house of Nazareth. However, from the number of scratches and burns thus far, I am evidently not doing things quite as well as Mary did.

You have been in my prayers during these busy days. Please keep praying that your daughter will become a perfect Carmelite. Jesus bless you, Mary guide, Joseph protect you!

Your loving daughter,
"Sister" Marie

P.S. Since Lent will begin this week, I shall not write again until Easter, but you will have a special place in all my Lenten prayers and penances.

Letter Thirteen

*D*earest Mother, Dad, and all my loved ones,
        "He is risen, alleluia!"

May our dear Savior's peace fill your souls and abide with you always. This is my fervent prayer for you on this happiest Easter of my life. How I wish you could experience the peace and joy of Easter in Carmel. It must be the dear Lord's gift for what we gave Him during the holy season of Lent.

Yes, Lent is rigorous—strict fasting according to the ancient usage of the Church had me quite hungry and somewhat more tired than usual.[27] We spent many days of prayer that brought us close to our suffering Redeemer. A day of recollection for the novices on the first Sunday of Lent was a fitting preparation for the holy season.

We had our Forty Hours Devotion on the second Sunday, during which three days of fervent prayer to our Eucharistic King I recommended each one of you. I was so happy that Sis's birthday coincided with the third day of the Forty Hours. If prohibitions against letter writing during Lent prevented my sending a card, the

---

[27] The current norms for the Lenten Fast are followed.

day spent with Jesus let me send many, many prayerful greetings to the "best sister in the whole world."

We were privileged to have a three-day retreat preached by our Carmelite provincial. What days of grace these were as Father explained to us the Carmelite method of prayer and showed us ways through which we might attain to our goal—union with God. On Laetare Sunday, the professed sisters had their day of recollection, so we novices did all the work. We really did have to move fast to finish dinner on time and then wash all the dishes; but the gratitude of our older sisters amply repaid our day's work.

During that and the following weeks, I prayed very earnestly for you so that each one of you would acquire all the graces that a mission can give. On Passion Sunday, all the sisters of the Iron Mountain deanery were invited to Carmel for a day of recollection. As we listened to Father's very instructive and inspiring conferences on the "Steps to Heaven," I was praying that your mission preacher was helping you as much as Father helped us. His Reverence made it so clear that our faith, obedience, love of God, and love of neighbor are steps we take, things we do—that is, we will to believe, to obey, to love regardless of feelings.

But these were only preparations for the great week—Holy Week. As we moved about the monastery in even stricter silence (not even broken for recreation during this week according to a custom of the original house of the Reform in Ávila, Spain), I was overwhelmed with sorrow for the giddy waste of precious time I had made in the past. No wonder you used to shake your heads, Dad and Mother, as Sis and I spent Holy Week arranging our Easter finery.

Here the arranging was so different: we wove and braided palms to decorate the altar for Palm Sunday; we spent hours baking tiny loaves of bread that were blessed on Holy Thursday for distribution to all who visited our chapel.

Oh, how beautiful the repository was: set high up in the corner of the sanctuary, our dear Lord's throne was decorated with a taste that inspired me. As I looked through the grate during the many hours of that sacred night and day (we are permitted to stay in Choir the whole of Holy Thursday night if we can), white and gold glistened in the flicker of many long tapers. The lilies, your gift, were so close to Jesus, reminding Him of your love and pleading for His blessing on your lives. No other gift could have made me so happy. We had the *Mandatum* or Washing of Feet on Holy Thursday. How solemn was this ceremony during which our Reverend Mother washed our feet while we chanted the beautiful canticle: "Where charity and love are, there is God." Surely God *is* here.

Good Friday—we went about our tasks in absolute silence, a solemn mourning pervading the cloister. Bread and water was our only food on this day of days, and as we took the meager repast, a sister knelt in the center of the refectory with a large cross on her Charity's shoulders. We spent the "three hours" just as you did—in meditation on the Passion. Then we venerated the relic of the True Cross, a treasured gift from our good bishop.[28]

A statue of our dear Lord in death placed before a bare cross kept us mindful all day Holy Saturday of Mary's grief. What joy filled our souls, however, on Saturday evening as the bells pealed and the organ swelled to the joyous message of the *Gloria!* We notice the dearth of bells more than you, for our life is regulated by a series of bells, all of which are replaced with the deathlike rattle on Holy Thursday. Easter brought such joys: the glorious alleluias of the liturgy; the sisterly embraces of our companions; the simple, happy feast.

It brought your letters, too, and after six weeks of not hearing from you, this was a real joy. All the sisters enjoyed the candy as you can be sure I did. May Jesus bless you for adding these joys to my already happy Easter. As you shared in my prayers and penances of Lent, so will you share in my prayers of this joyous Paschaltide. Jesus and Mary bless and keep you.

Your loving daughter,
"Sister" Marie

---

[28] The liturgy of the Sacred Triduum is observed according to the revised Roman Missal, including the Mass of the Lord's Supper on Holy Thursday, the Good Friday liturgy, and the Easter Vigil Mass on Saturday night.

Letter Fourteen

$\mathcal{D}$earest Mother, Dad, and all my loved ones,

Pax Christi, alleluia! His glorious victory be your constant source of peace!

The Paschaltide joys that are so real in Carmel were heightened the other day when I witnessed the ceremony of temporary profession. I know you will be anxious to hear all the details of a "profession day" in Carmel.[29]

No one minded the darkness that morning when the alarm sounded at 4:30 a.m. — each one in our family shares so intimately and so completely in the joys of the others. It was Sister Therese's great day, the day of her espousals. As we entered the Novitiate oratory, we were thrilled: soft candlelight revealed the beautifully decorated altar with Mary reigning as Queen amidst flowers and candles; the lovely Infant Jesus in His glass-enclosed niche reached out His arms from the glistening white satin and lace dress as if to draw His little bride close to His Heart. We knelt as the whole community, clothed in white mantles and long veils,

---

[29] The profession as here described is now required to take place at Mass. Family members may attend.

assembled in the oratory. Each of us carried a candle, and at a signal we formed into a procession, at the head of which one sister carried the Crucifix. Sister Therese walked last in line with our Mother. As we made our way through the cloister to the Choir, we chanted the beautiful hymn "O Gloriosa Virginum" in honor of our Blessed Mother.

When we entered the Choir, we were again thrilled by the simple but expressive decorations. At the end of the hymn, Sister went to the center of the Choir and, kneeling there, listened to the beautiful exhortation that our Mother gave concerning the vows. I wish I could remember all that her Reverence said, but perhaps this little I can remember will help you understand the vows as it helped me.

"Arise," her Reverence said, "cut the cords that have heretofore bound you to the world, creatures, and self. Arise and let your voice be heard in our land—Carmel. Arise from things of earth to those of Heaven by your vow of poverty, for having left all things for His love, your soul can cry out 'all things are mine for Christ is mine' (St. John of the Cross). Arise through your vow of chastity to a love divine, to an intimacy with God that will keep growing as your love becomes more pure and disinterested. Arise by your vow of obedience to the sovereignty of a queen truly mistress over self. Fear not to nail yourself with Christ to His Cross: the vows will bind you only to make you free; burden you but only with His sweet yoke; 'bleed' you only to make you perfect.

"Give yourself, then, for truly when a Religious binds herself, it is more a receiving than a giving. Never cheat the Lord in thought, word, or deed: He called and you answered; He desired and you responded; He loved and now your Charity must love and love. Poverty will enrich you with His inheritance; chastity make you the source of life in other souls for whom you pray and sacrifice;

obedience assure you of an unerring path to perfection. The more fully you give to God, the more fully you shall receive for yourself and for all for whom you pray. We are destined to supply the 'arms' for the battle to save souls.... We are destined to 'mother' souls for Christ."

I forgot to mention before that Sister Therese carried a large, beautifully adorned candle in her right hand and the handwritten formula of profession in her left. These her Charity held during the exhortation, at the end of which our Mother Mistress took the candle. Then Sister, placing her hands in those of our Mother and holding at the same time the formula of her profession, pronounced her temporary vows: "I, Sister Therese, make my profession of temporary vows for three years, and I promise obedience, chastity, and poverty to God, to the Most Blessed Virgin Mary of Mount Carmel, and to you, Reverend Mother Prioress, and to your successors, according to the Primitive *Rule* of the Order of Discalced Carmelites and our *Constitutions*."

Next our Mother gave her Charity each of the blessed parts of the holy Habit—the cincture (or leather belt), the Scapular, and the white choir mantle.[30] As soon as the prayers were said, Sister prostrated. (That means her Charity lay flat on the floor with arms extended to form a cross.) Her Charity remained thus prostrate as we chanted the glorious hymn of triumph—"Te Deum Laudamus"—and answered the many invocations and prayers that our Mother chanted. How beautiful these are as they plead for grace for the newly professed that her life may be, in the words of our saintly Sister Elizabeth of the Trinity, "a praise of glory to the Most Blessed Trinity."

---

[30] This part is no longer part of the profession ceremony but belongs to the reception of the Habit and initiation into the Novitiate.

At the end of these prayers Sister arose and received the Crucifix for her Rosary as also one to wear on her breast. Then, crowned with a wreath of white roses, Sister came to embrace each of us, asking our prayers. During this ceremony we chanted: "*Ecce quam bonum* ... Behold how good and how pleasant it is for brethren to dwell together in unity."

My heart still thrills as I remember that happy day. A solemn Mass with an inspiring sermon was the climax. Since the profession is strictly private, the family can participate in this part of the celebration and then spend the day visiting at the grate with the newly professed sister.

The sisters told me that solemn profession is even more inspiring. The ceremony, they said, is the same as that for simple vows, only the words of the profession formula are different: "I make my solemn profession and I promise ... until death."

Another difference is that when the sister prostrates after pronouncing her solemn vows, her Charity is covered with a black pall—symbolic of her death to the world.[31] I forgot to mention above that when Sister Therese prostrated after pronouncing her simple vows, flower petals were strewn over her—symbolic of the virtues that her Charity must learn to practice.

Then, too, after the solemn profession, the sister's wreath has long thorns interwoven with the flowers. But the biggest difference is that the sister who makes solemn vows receives from the bishop, at the public ceremony that takes place during Mass,

---

[31] This detail is no longer practiced. During the current ceremony for solemn profession, which takes place during Mass, the sister prostrates during the singing of the Litany. The newly professed nun is crowned with a wreath of white roses as a symbol of her virginal union with Christ.

the black veil that is the exterior mark of her "nuptials with the Lamb."

How I long for "my day of espousal"! Please pray that I may be found worthy. May our Risen Lord fill your souls with joy!

Your loving daughter,
"Sister" Marie

Letter Fifteen

*D*earest Mother, Dad, and all,

  May Jesus reign in your hearts always!

Your enthusiasm about Carmel's profession ceremony gives me so much encouragement—actually you seem to be as anxious for your Carmelite's profession as she is! Your generosity in this matter will surely draw down on you God's very special blessings. Oh, if you only knew how many poor girls are deprived of the joy of serving God in Carmel because of parental opposition. How can I ever thank you enough for considering my call to Carmel a real family blessing? But before looking ahead to the profession, you must beg our dear Lord to let me receive the holy Habit that is the first step.

Never having witnessed a clothing ceremony, I cannot give any description of its details; but I can try to resume the explanations we received concerning the meaning of each part of the holy Habit. *Penance and dedication to God through His Immaculate Mother*—these are the clues to why Carmelites dress as they do. Our holy Mother, St. Teresa of Ávila, left us a clear description of what our holy Habit should be; so with only a few minor variations in the arrangement of the headdress (a point not specifically mentioned by our holy Mother), all Carmelites dress the same.

Our title, *Discalced* Carmelite Nuns, is descriptive of one phase of our dress. (Here I keep saying "our" Habit not because I wear these things but because I trust that very soon Our Lord will permit me to exchange the postulant's garb for the holy Habit of Carmel.) The term really means *barefooted* Carmelites, and that is precisely what we are. The sisters make the "alpargates," or rope-soled sandals, by braiding common rope and winding it to form a sole. Then woven tops are affixed to hold the soles on one's feet. The stockings that our holy Mother counsels us to wear "for decency" have no feet in them but are held down by a strap that goes under the instep. This kind of footwear, although somewhat resembling modern toeless and heel-less play shoes, is used in Carmel to eliminate both vanity and noise. Surely the absolute shapelessness of the homemade and oft-mended sandals accomplishes the first aim, while the flat hemp soles do help the sisters to walk very quietly.

My work making and mending Habits has acquainted me with the various parts. It is somewhat of a penance, I imagine, to wear the white woolen undergarment that is called a "tunic." Coarse brown serge is used for the Habit (or outer tunic), which is quite easy to make since it hangs straight down from the shoulder and has straight, wide sleeves set in without any gathers, darts, or pleats.[32] The blessing of this Habit is so inspiring, as is, too, the prayer with which it is given to the sister at her "clothing": "May the Lord clothe thee with the new man who is created according to God in justice and holiness of truth."

---

[32] According to the 1990 *Constitutions*, other materials may be used to sew the Habits as former fabrics are not always available or are difficult to acquire.

A leather cincture is worn over the Habit, a constant reminder to the Carmelite that "she may not walk where she would (as in her former way of life) but that now another has bound her and will lead her (through obedience) where (naturally speaking) she would not"—along the thorny way to perfection. The coif or head covering is made of very coarse linen and is never starched. The novices' white veils are also of linen, whereas the professed sisters have the additional penance of black woolen veils.

The Scapular is worn over the coif. This is the most significant part of the holy Habit—actually it *is* the Habit of Carmel. It consists of two long panels of the same coarse brown serge, one of which falls down the front, the other down the back. These are joined together by two brown serge shoulder straps. This is the *livery of Mary, the clothing of the Mother of God* that is so highly indulgenced. I told you before about the Scapular of Carmel and how *you* can wear an abbreviated form of this wonderful gift from Heaven. Are you wearing your Brown Scapular? When it is placed on the sister's shoulders for the first time, the bishop bids her, "Take upon thee the yoke of Christ, which is sweet, and the burden which is light." It thrills me to see the sisters reverently kiss their Scapulars and carefully arrange them so as not to kneel or sit on this precious sacramental.

A large rosary hangs from the cincture on the left side, thus completing the Habit. There is one more detail that will show how we practice poverty and avoid vanity—the handkerchief. I was so surprised the first time I saw the brown-checked cotton handkerchiefs that replace sparkling white linen ones in our cloister.

At all solemn functions, for example a clothing or profession ceremony as well as at the daily conventual Mass at which we receive Holy Communion, the sisters wear the beautiful white choir mantle. It is made of serge and is about three inches shorter than the Habit.

The Communion veil is worn in such a way that it hangs over the back of the mantle. This is wool, too, white for the novices and black for the professed sisters. It really makes a lovely picture when the sisters are in the Choir and makes me long more and more to be clothed as they are—holy envy surely, but I do not think it is really wrong. The prayer recited as the sister receives the mantle is a summary of why we live this life of total dedication: "They who follow the Lamb without spot shall walk with Him in white; may therefore thy vesture be ever white as a sign of thy inner purity." To walk with the Lamb, with Jesus—clothed in the livery of His own Virgin Mother—can there be a more wonderful goal in life?

The letter is so long already, and the time for writing is just about over, so I shall close with a plea for your prayers. Beg Jesus and Mary to make me worthy of every one of Carmel's gifts and graces.

Your loving daughter,
"Sister" Marie

"The livery of Mary, —

the clothing of the Mother of God."

Letter Sixteen

*D*earest Mother, Dad, and all my loved ones,
     Praised be Jesus Christ!

How did you fix the May altar this year, Mother? It was so beautiful last year. I can remember how Dad supplied the fresh flowers by getting them from the greenhouse during the weeks after that unusually heavy frost had spoiled all the spring flowers in the garden. Oh, how it must please our Blessed Mother when the whole family gathers at her shrine to pray the Rosary and Litany. Please remember us in your prayers.

Here in Carmel we, too, have daily May devotions: the Rosary, the Litany, several hymns, and Benediction of the Most Blessed Sacrament. I do not know whether it is because I love our Blessed Mother so much or because it reminds me so much of home—but the May devotions give me real joy. Another special "May devotion" in Carmel brings us very close to Mary. Before her statue in the Choir, a beautifully decorated basket is placed amid flowers and candles. Each day we try to perform as many acts of virtue, mortification, and self-denial as possible, which acts we mark on a little slip of paper. The sisters vie with one another to see who can put the most slips in the basket, for we know that Mary makes good use of the sacrifices and prayers that we offer her by applying them to the salvation of souls. Of course, our Blessed Mother is the only "scorekeeper," so we shall not know who did the most until Eternity.

Speaking of offerings to Mary reminds me, Mother dear, of the offerings I shall make for you on Mother's Day. This is the second time lately that your birthday coincided with that day already set aside in your honor. The little enclosed card is for you to open that day; its contents, the first result of my efforts at painting. However it looks to others, it will mean much to you. You will have a triduum of prayers before the great day, and the card tells the rest of the gift from your Carmelite.

You know, May is not the only time we honor Mary in Carmel. Since we are especially designated "the children of the Blessed Virgin Mary of Mount Carmel" and are clothed with her livery, our lives are filled with devotion to Mary. Each of her feasts is a day of rejoicing, and on most of the greater ones, we solemnly chant parts of the Divine Office instead of simply reciting them. The Gregorian chant, at once so simple and so solemn, is a fitting praise for her who, while so simple and humble, is so wonderfully exalted. The joyous feast of July 16, which honors Mary as the Queen of Carmel, is one of the happiest in our Carmelite year.

As we close each day's hours of prayer and work, we salute Mary with the beautiful antiphon in her honor. This is a practice of the universal Church, for the hour of Compline, the night prayer of Holy Mother Church, closes with this salutation to Mary. In Carmel, we chant whichever antiphon is in season. The *Alma Redemptoris Mater* in Advent, the *Ave Regina* in Lent, *Regina Coeli* in Paschaltide, and *Salve Regina* during the rest of the year. Can you not imagine what joy this gives our Blessed Mother?

Each Saturday we chant the votive Mass in honor of our Blessed Lady of Mount Carmel. It is a new thrill each week and a fresh

opportunity to recommend priests, loved ones, and all our friends
to the care of this wonderful Mother. If there is a great feast on
Saturday, we anticipate the votive Mass on the Friday—Holy Week
being the only exception to this general rule.

One of the most beautiful of Carmel's ceremonies takes place
each Saturday evening. At the signal of the large bell, all the sisters,
wearing white mantles and carrying lighted candles, assemble in
the corridor outside the Choir. Then, when the organ intones the
solemn march, we enter slowly and reverently. Making the genuflec-
tion two by two in the front of the Choir, we then go to our places
on the sides. Oh, it is so beautiful—the white mantles symbolic

of Mary's purity, the flickering tapers telling of her wonderful holiness. After the whole community has entered the Choir, the solemn *Salve Regina* is intoned! "Hail ... hail holy Queen," and we bow low in homage to her who reigns as the Mother of Mercy. On through the praises of our Mother we joyously sing, the Gregorian melody swelling to heights of beauty as it proclaims her beauty and splendor. On the eves of our Blessed Mother's feasts, we also have the solemn *Salve*, before which we have "the letter of bondage." This is an act of consecration to our Blessed Mother much like the one composed by St. Louis Marie de Montfort. Each feast, a different sister, chosen by lot, has the privilege of reading the act of consecration. As we kneel, candle in hand, we unite with her Charity in offering ourselves again to Mary. Oh, I hope you are here visiting some Saturday evening so that you can be in the chapel for the *Salve Regina* solemnly chanted.

Another privilege here is to be assigned "the Chaplainess of the Blessed Virgin." This office is changed each week, and as each sister has her turn, her Charity tries to prove in countless ways her love for Mary. That week we may decorate her shrines as the outward proof of our love; but above all, we can, by imitating her love for Jesus, adorn our hearts and make them shrines in her honor. Oh, Mother and Dad, you would love Carmel as I do if you could participate in these acts of love for Mary. But why say "if you"? You can by joining your own day's work, prayer, joys, and trials to our acts of homage to Mary. Clothed as you are in her Scapular, you are one with all of us in Carmel.

May she bend lovingly over each of you and protect you!

Your loving daughter,
"Sister" Marie

Letter Seventeen

*D*ear Mother, Dad, and all my loved ones,
Praised be Jesus Christ! May His wonderful peace fill your souls!

After this letter it will be a month before I write again. This is the custom, our Mother said, to which exception can, of course, be made in case of necessity. I am very sorry to be such a source of distress to you—for I understand how hard it is to listen to well-meaning friends' objections to a "cloistered vocation." Just the other day during dinner, a passage from the *Liturgical Year* made me perk up and listen in a special way. The saintly and scholarly Benedictine, Abbot Gueranger, gave a very pointed answer to these objectors that will solve your doubts:

> To those who would fain hold them back, when on the threshold of the religious state, under pretense of the great good they may do in the world and how much evil they may prevent. Just as though the Most High must be contented with useless nonentities among those He chooses; or, as though the aptitudes of the most gifted natures may not be turned all the better and all the more completely to God,

their very principle, precisely because they are the most perfect. On the other hand, neither State nor Church ever really loses anything by this fleeing to God, this apparent throwing away of the best subjects!

So, Mother and Dad, do not feel that I am burying my talents or wasting the education your sacrifices made possible. In Carmel they will be sublimated—raised to a new dignity; for, instead of procuring the passing satisfaction of praise for me, they will glorify the Infinite God. They are His by right—mine only through His condescension. The more I hear about our holy Order, the more thoroughly I am convinced that however talented we may seem to be, we shall have to strive earnestly even to follow (at a great distance) in the footsteps of the saintly Carmelites who have preceded us.

You know, the Order of Carmel is so ancient that it precedes the Christian era. The hermits who were its founders lived long before the coming of Christ on Mount Carmel in Palestine. The holy prophets, St. Elias, called our founder, and St. Eliseus,[33] gathered many followers around them and, there on the Mount of Carmel, adored God in "spirit and in truth." Their example has lived on in the members of our holy Order.

Now please tell all those who harass you with objections to your daughter's being in Carmel that you know she has found peace and happiness. What more could any parent desire for a

---

[33] St. Elijah and St. Elisha have traditionally been honored as saints in the Carmelite Order. The feast day of St. Elijah is July 20. St. Elisha's feast day, formerly June 14, is no longer observed in the new missal. Both holy prophets of the Old Testament are highly honored in the East. This devotion was bought to the West with the Carmelites.

child! Tell them, too, that since she aspires to become "the bride of Christ," you have no worries about her future.

You have very special mementos in my daily prayers. Now that letters will be fewer, I shall make the prayers even more.

Your loving daughter,
"Sister" Marie

CARMEL'S PRAYER~ AS INCENSE ASCENDS TO HEAVEN.

Letter Eighteen

*D*ear Mother, Dad, and all,

     May the Queen of Carmel bend lovingly over each one of you, thus drawing you ever closer to her Divine Son!

It seems that one sentence of the last letter has you "amazed." We really are Catholic here in Carmel, even if our holy Order had its beginning in the Old Testament era. Here is a little résumé of our history. As you know, Carmel is a mountain in Palestine, mentioned frequently in the Bible because of its extraordinary beauty. Nine hundred years before the birth of our dear Lord, this holy mount was the dwelling place of St. Elias, the great prophet whose mighty works fill many pages of Scripture. It is from this holy father, whose descendants we are, that we have received our watchword: *Zelo zelatus sum pro Domine Deo exercituum* ("With zeal have I been zealous for the Lord God of hosts").

Under the leadership of St. Elias, the hermits, living in the caverns and forests of Carmel, gathered to lead a common life of prayer, penance, and celibacy. Dating from the vision granted to St. Elias wherein he saw the Virgin Mother of the promised Savior prefigured by a little cloud rising out of the sea,[34] the hermits of Carmel were most devoted to the Mother of God who was to come.

When St. John the Baptist preached the baptism of penance, the hermits then living on Carmel became his disciples. On the first Pentecost, these Carmelites embraced the Christian religion, becoming followers of and co-workers with the apostles. A pious tradition tells that the Blessed Mother actually visited these holy men in their isolated hermitages; and it is an authentic fact that as early as the year 85 A.D., the first chapel ever built in Mary's honor was erected on Carmel. Because of this exceeding love of the Mother of God, the hermits were called "the Brothers of Our Lady of Mount Carmel."

During the Crusades, when Christians went to fight the Saracens in the Holy Land, many, struck by the evident holiness of the monks on Carmel, joined their ranks. Gradually, the Order spread into Western Europe, and when the persecution of Christians in the Holy Land became extremely violent, most of the Carmelites migrated westward.

More troubles awaited the Brothers in Europe. Recent Church regulations having declared that no new orders were to be founded, there were objections to this new monastic family. The situation became such that there was real danger of the Order's being suppressed, but the Blessed Virgin appeared to Pope Honorius III, warning his Holiness to take under his protection this Order that bore her name. Mary also bade the pope to favor "her Order" by confirming its *Rule*, title, and privileges. Thus Mary saved our holy Order from dissolution, but troubles continued.

---

[34] This interpretation comes from an old Carmelite work entitled *The Institution of the First Monks*, which sees in the small cloud seen by Elijah a foreshadowing of Mary and her Immaculate Conception.

Letter Eighteen

On July 16, 1251, the Blessed Mother showed a new sign of her maternal love. St. Simon Stock, General of the Order, placing his entire confidence in Mary, asked her to give some visible sign of her protection. The "Scapular Vision," during which our Blessed Mother gave to the saint the Habit (Scapular) of the Order, was Mary's answer:

> "This will be the sign of the privileges which I have obtained for thee and for the children of Carmel: whoever dies (piously) clothed with this Habit will be preserved from eternal flames."

This is the promise of Mary, and you can share in it. Do you remember reading how our Blessed Mother appeared again at Fatima as Our Lady of Mount Carmel? She so ardently desires to clothe us with her protecting livery! Only since my entrance into Carmel have I begun to realize the wonderful privileges attached to wearing the Brown Scapular—and I want to share these with you. Please, if you do not yet wear the Brown Scapular, begin to do so always.

When I told our Mother that this letter was more or less a history book, her Reverence laughed. "Well, I trust your Charity told your loved ones the best part of our history—the facts about the Brown Scapular," her Reverence said. Then our Mother added, "We better enclose one of these leaflets and a Scapular in this letter."

That really gave me great joy. It makes a wonderful gift for Dad for Father's Day. A little extra note will enumerate the spiritual bouquet that his Carmelite sends for that day. But now this letter must close, so I leave you with the best of all mothers, and beg her to lead you very close to the Heart of her Divine Son.

Your loving daughter,
"Sister" Marie

Letter Nineteen

*D*earest Mother, Dad, and all my loved ones,
"In the heart of my Mother, the Church, I will be love."
Thus did little St. Thérèse express the fervent desire of every Carmelite — her desire to please God, sanctify herself, and save souls by hidden acts of love.

Although the last letter told you about the origin of the Carmelite Order, it did not mention how or when the nuns actually began — and this mystery you are anxious to have solved. I think the following will answer your questions. There are some documents that prove that there were nuns in Palestine before the Fathers migrated into Europe, others that show the existence of isolated communities of nuns in Europe as early as 1261. But the real organization of the Carmelite Nuns is attributed to Bl. John Soreth, who became the General of the Order in 1451. Monasteries of nuns were established during and after his time in many European countries including Belgium, France, Germany, and Spain.

During the terrible plagues of the Black Death that swept over Europe, the religious orders lost hundreds of members. Carmelites found it impossible to observe the severe Rule of St. Albert that enjoined perpetual abstinence and fasting for the greater part of the year. Hence, the Order petitioned the Holy Father for some dispensations. Pope Eugenius, in 1430, granted that the Rule be mitigated: abstinence was no longer perpetual; the number of fast days was lessened; and the religious were no longer bound to such strict retirement. This mitigated Rule was also adopted by the nuns, not through laxity but because of the weakened condition of society after the plague.

In 1515, Teresa de Ahumada was born in Ávila, Spain. When eighteen years old, she entered the Carmelite monastery in Ávila, where she spent twenty years preparing herself by prayer, penance, and obedience for the great work God had destined her to do. Moved by divine inspiration, she, whom we lovingly call our holy Mother, established her reform.

It is from this "reform" that the Discalced Carmelites take their origin—their first monastery being that of St. Joseph in Ávila, which was founded in 1562 by the saint. From this time the Discalced Carmelites followed the primitive Rule of St. Albert, which enjoins perpetual abstinence from meat, fasting during the greater part of the year, and a strictly cloistered life of silence, penance, and prayer.

Our holy Mother, St. Teresa, gave a summary of her ardent desire to help Holy Mother Church in the reasons for undertaking this gigantic task of the reform:

> Hearing of the miseries and disorders caused by those Lutherans[35] ... I resolved to do the little in my power; that is, to follow the evangelical counsels with all the perfection I could and induce the few nuns here to do the same ... that all of us being engaged in prayer for the champions (priests)

[35] St. Teresa lived at the time of the Protestant Reformation. At times, such as in this case, she is probably referring to the Huguenots in France.

of the Church, we might—to the utmost of our power—assist my Lord who has been so much insulted by those for whom He has done so much. (*The Way of Perfection*, chap. 1, par. 2 —written by herself)

You see, Mother and Dad, our main work is *prayer for priests*. Oh, yes, we pray for all who recommend themselves to us, but we are, as one of the diocesan priests recently wrote, "the priests' silent partners in saving souls—silent partners in the eyes of the world but atomic blasts at the foot of God's throne," where our hidden acts of sacrifice and love obtain wonderful graces for souls.

I hope this has answered your questions. Just in case there are still some doubts in your mind, our Mother gave me permission to send you the book *Carmel, Its History, Spirit, and Saints*, which will give you more information. You know I never was an outstanding history student; so my brief résumé probably lacks many interesting details.

However, the history of our holy Order does fascinate me. It is thrilling to read of the saints who preceded us—and it is a real challenge. Please beg God to let your daughter follow in the footsteps of these saintly men and women as perfectly as possible.

May God reward you, Mother, for the box of sewing supplies. The thimble fits perfectly; so our Mother allowed me to keep it. The other things are in the common box; so you have the grateful prayers of all the novices.

Time to go now. May Jesus and His wonderful Mother, Mary, love and bless each one of you.

Your loving daughter,
"Sister" Marie

Let nothing
disturb thee,
nothing affright thee.
All things are passing.
God never changes.
Patience gains all things.
Who has God
wants nothing.
God alone suffices.

— Saint Teresa's Bookmark

Letter Twenty

*D*ear Mother, Dad, and all,
     "The Father seeketh submission; suffering draweth the Son; but the Holy Spirit by silence alone is won."

You do not understand what my reference to "our life of silence" meant; hence, it has naturally upset your peace of soul. It is not an abnormal condition that, as certain persons evidently have told you, can only lead to nervous tension or other psychological difficulties.

My own clumsy way of saying things could never describe the beauty of Carmel's silence. For that reason, I shall tell you how some of our saints and holy Carmelites have described it. The Primitive Rule itself enjoins silence and quotes Scripture to show the excellence of this injunction: "He that uses idle words shall hurt his own soul"; "in *silence* and hope shall your strength be"; "on the day of judgment, you will render an account of every idle word which you have spoken."[36] This is the encomium of the Holy Spirit. Can there be a better authority? Our holy father, St. John

---

[36] Sister Marie is paraphrasing and combining two different passages from Scripture here: Matthew 12:36–37 and Isaiah 30:15.

of the Cross, succinctly remarked, "A soul that is easily inclined to talk and converse is but little inclined toward God." Another holy Carmelite remarked, "It is silence that prepares saints; silence that begins, continues, and perfects the life of sanctity."

The "Great Silence," which is observed by almost all religious communities, begins after Compline each evening and lasts until after Prime the following morning.[37] Except in very rare instances or emergencies, the sisters should not break this silence. During the day we are cautioned to speak only when necessity or charity demands it, and then to limit ourselves to as few words as possible. "If two words will suffice, we owe Our Lord the obligation of not using three," says an ancient *Book of Customs*. The novices are strictly forbidden to speak to anyone except the Novice Mistress and the Reverend Mother Prioress.[38]

I know that hearing these things is causing you concern, but just read on patiently and I hope that you will soon agree with us about the beauty of this silence. Did you ever walk alone through the beautiful woods behind our house? Do you not recall how, as you walked, looking at the beauty of the trees, the sky, the tiny flowers, you were not lonely? You could *think*—think about the beauties you were seeing and about the Infinite One whose works they are. Bunnies and chipmunks, red birds and flickers came so very close to you when you were silent—and this thrilled you too.

Well, that is how we enjoy silence. We go through the monastery, carefully guarding our eyes against distractions so that we can look at our Infinite God. We avoid useless chatter so that our minds

---

[37] With the suppression of Prime, the Great Silence lasts until after Lauds in the morning.

[38] The novices are permitted to ask necessary questions during their work. They take part in the community recreations twice a day, according to the family spirit of Carmel.

can be filled with Him—with His infinite love. We work as quietly as possible, walk as softly as we can so that we avoid disturbing our sisters. It is not negative at all; not a constant repression but very positive—a seeking for the One we love.

The silence is broken at noon and in the evening when we gather for the hour of recreation. These are happy moments. You will never hear gaiety so real in any worldly circle. There, as we recount some of the funny incidents that have happened or share with one another some particularly interesting reading, we find relaxation. "Carmelites are the happiest people I have ever seen." This was my first reaction, and it is each new sister's first impression. The simplicity of our life helps us to find happiness in everything.

You probably wonder if there is not some way to convey messages since we do not speak during the day. Yes, we have a "sign language." Each sister is taught the fundamental and most-often-used signs. Then, as occasion arises, we use our ingenuity to convey a message that has no established sign. Sometimes these are really funny, but usually we make each other understand without too much difficulty. Several times, as I am still quite slow, a sister looked at me and rubbed her thumb on the tips of the index and middle fingers. I thought that her Charity must have had something sticky on her fingers and was rubbing it off. I surely was surprised to find out later that it was the sign that said, "Go quickly!"

Another time a sister made a motion as if her Charity were drinking and then pointed to a two-quart milk bottle that had a little bit of milk left in it. Not knowing that this meant for me to put a little bit of water in the bottle to rinse out the remaining milk, thus avoiding waste, I put the two-quart bottle to my mouth and drank the milk. Sister's look of amazement told me that I had misunderstood the sign.

My own look of amazement when the final-professed sister, who is sacristan, came to me and struck her breast caused some confusion. That is a sign having two meanings: (1) a means of acknowledging one's fault, which meaning I knew; and (2) the sign that the confessor is here, which I did not know. Sister was calling me to Confession; and there I was, confused and embarrassed, trying to make her Charity understand by other signs that she had done nothing to offend me. Now, thanks be to God, I can understand and make signs quite easily.

You see, there is nothing to worry about with regard to our silence. It is the silence of God—the most effective means of finding peace and real joy. Our little Sister Elizabeth of the Trinity, the saintly French Carmelite, summed it up well in these words: "Beneath the Divine Touch, oh remain in silence, so that the Image of the Savior may be imprinted on your soul."

Do not worry. I love our silence more each day.

Your loving daughter,
"Sister" Marie

Letter Twenty-One

*D*ear Mother, Dad, and all my loved ones,
　　　　May the peace of Christ remain in your souls!
You must be patient with your Carmelite. There are so many things she wants to tell you about Carmel, but it will take a little while. The word "Choir" seems to confuse you. Maybe, if I try to describe it, you will be able to picture that most lovely spot in our monastery.

As you know, we are strictly cloistered, which means that we never go out of that part of the monastery that is reserved for us—the cloister. Hence, we do not go into the public chapel at all, not even to assist at Holy Mass. We have our own little section of the chapel, entirely separated from and yet actually a part of the public chapel. This section is called the Choir.

"How," you will ask, "can the Choir be separated from but a part of the chapel?" Well, across the front of the Choir there is a large opening. This opening is covered on the sanctuary side by a grill or grate, while on our side there are vertical bars about two inches apart the whole length of the opening. The space between the grate and the bars is the thickness of the wall—through which is drawn a black curtain.

Inside the Cloistered Life

We make mental prayer, assist at Holy Mass and Benediction, and make our visits to the Blessed Sacrament looking through the curtain and the grates. Many persons think this must be a sacrifice, but it is not. As one of our very saintly Carmelites so well expressed it: "I am ever more fond of the dear grilles (grates) that make me His prisoner of love. I like to think how we are prisoners, each for the other" (Sister Elizabeth of the Trinity).

In the center of the grate is a small window that is unlocked only during Mass and other very special functions. We receive Holy Communion by kneeling, one by one, at this little window. It is through this window, too, that our good bishop gives the holy Habit of Carmel to the religious and the black veil to the final professed nun. We receive the blessed ashes on Ash Wednesday and palm on Palm Sunday here; and on February 3, feast of St. Blaise, we have our throats blessed at this same window. You see, it is for us what the Communion railing is in church.

Now to describe the rest of the Choir. Its austere beauty may be hard to picture, but I shall try. As one enters the Choir and genuflects, she is facing the grate through which can be seen the dim outline of the altar. Oh, it is so thrilling to kneel there close to the grate—so very close to the tabernacle! There is a large, very devotional Crucifix above the Communion window—that is, in the center of the grate.

Our stalls—the name of the individual seats—are lined along each side wall with the seats turned to the center of the Choir. The Stations of the Cross are on the walls somewhat above the tops of the stalls. We kneel in front of the stalls, right on the floor, since there are no kneelers or prie-dieux. This kneeling on the floor is sometimes quite hard on the new sisters, but gradually one's knees become accustomed to the penance.

Right now we are so squeezed that we practically kneel on the toes of the sister in front of us. One sister jokingly suggested making a hole in the baseboard of the back wall so that her feet could go into the space between the walls. We have quite a time during the evening Asperges (sprinkling with holy water). The sister who sprinkles us has to step over the feet of one sister, while another tries to squeeze her feet as far under the stall as possible in order to give more room for passing. The close quarters give us many occasions of suffering inconvenience, and at the same time they afford many amusing incidents.[39]

At the back of the Choir is an altar on which the candles are lit for the Divine Office. We had to replace the altar with a small pedestal to make room. Our Reverend Mother and Mother Sub-Prioress kneel between their stalls, which face the front of the Choir, and the pedestal. Right in the center of the back wall, above the pedestal, is a beautiful statue of our Blessed Mother. It is traditional in Carmel to place an image of Mary near the Prioress's stall, because Mary is really our superior. Every Carmelite Prioress places her power in the hands of this loving Mother, asking Mary to direct her words and actions for the good of the souls entrusted to her care.

Statues of the Sacred Heart, the Infant Jesus of Prague, and our father St. Joseph have their places of honor in our Choir. As I pass each one when making visits, I remind our dear Lord, His wonderful Mother, and His glorious foster father of each one of you at home.

That is a sketch of our Choir, incomplete surely; but it will give you some idea of what the word means. It is here, in this

---

[39] The reference to close quarters refers to the original building, a former hotel, that was used for the monastery at its foundation. In 1966, the community moved to the new monastery built on a beautiful stretch of land several miles north of Iron Mountain, where they are located to this day.

atmosphere of peace, that we recite the Divine Office, make mental prayer, and spend happy moments with our Eucharistic King.

Next week I shall spend many, many hours in Choir. My private eight-day retreat in preparation for "clothing" will begin on Friday night. Please beg Jesus and Mary to help me prepare well for that great occasion.

Dad's birthday will occur during those precious days; so I am enclosing a little something for him in this letter. Do not let Dad open it ahead of time, Mother, and please give him a big embrace on that day from his loving Carmelite. You will have a *big* gift of prayers that day especially sent to the best dad in all the world. It is time to close now. May Jesus keep each of you very close to His Sacred Heart.

Your loving daughter,
"Sister" Marie

Letter Twenty-Two

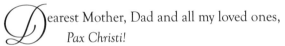earest Mother, Dad and all my loved ones,
   Pax Christi!

Oh, how that little phrase summarizes what I feel now that I am clothed in Carmel's Habit. The joy of that wonderful day was increased immeasurably by your presence here at Carmel. Did you experience the same thrill? Yes, I think you did, for your love makes you rejoice in your child's happiness.

You asked that I write some little account of the ceremony for Sis to relate at the sodality meeting. Nothing could please me more than to recount (relive) each of the precious moments of that morning. But to begin at the real starting point: My private retreat began eight days before the happy day. At the evening recreation on the first, I bade farewell to my Novitiate companions, begging their prayers that the forthcoming days be fruitful of much good in my soul. Our Mother Mistress gave me an *horarium* (schedule of how to spend the hours of the retreat days) and several very splendid spiritual reading books to help me meditate. Strict silence, absolute solitude—these were the helpful companions of the retreat, at the end of which I begged pardon, publicly, for all the mistakes and shortcomings of my months of postulancy. Then I had the wonderful privilege of making a general confession so that my soul might be prepared for the nuptials.

I do not remember if I thanked you for the bridal dress and accessories.[40] They were lovely and needed no alterations. I must confess, however, that it was a wee bit annoying to fuss with all the buttons and bobby pins after having accustomed myself to get along without them. The thought "This is the last time for all this vanity" made it easier. What a thrill it gave me when our Mother handed me your little ring, Mother dear, so that I could wear it for the occasion. Dad's gift of roses and lilies for the altars made me very happy. Some of the flowers were used for the Novitiate altar where Mary and the beautiful Infant Jesus were enshrined.

In the evening before the great day, our Mother summoned me to the recreation where, according to custom, I asked each nun for a spiritual alms. Each of my dear sisters offered me a share in her prayers and good works for a length of time. I felt so wonderfully fortified with this spiritual "dowry."

As you remember, Monsignor sang the early Mass. While the rest of the community took breakfast, I began to dress in the bridal finery. (I fasted until the Mass of the clothing.) It must have been about eight thirty that morning when everything was arranged,

---

[40] According to the new norms for the reception of the Habit and profession, the clothing ceremony is now private and much simpler. It is the mind of Holy Mother Church that the greater emphasis should be on the profession of vows, which is no longer private but takes place during the Holy Sacrifice of the Mass. The clothing is merely the initiation into the Novitiate, a time of training whereas the profession is comparable to a wedding—the nun becomes the spouse of Christ.

and all my loved sisters came to admire "the bride." Then I had the intense joy of going to the grate room to see and visit with you for the first time in so many months. Everyone looked so wonderful—your happiness increased the joy I already felt. Mother and Dad, I was so surprised to see that beautiful bridal cake you had ordered.

Our good bishop is such a father to us that his Excellency comes in person to give the holy Habit. (The ceremony could be delegated to another priest.) The bishop's Mass began at 9:30 a.m. To the solemn chanting of our Blessed Mother's *Magnificat*, the community in white mantles and long veils entered the Choir, with our Mother and "the bride" going last. At the end of the beautiful canticle, the sisters sang the "O Gloriosa Virginum" while I knelt on the prie-dieu in the front of the Choir. There I remained throughout the Mass, looking through the grate into the beautifully decorated sanctuary.

Our bishop's sermon, at once showing the sublimity of a "call to Carmel" and the grave responsibilities it entails, was like a trumpet call to my generosity. It made me conscious of my nothingness, of the condescension of the God who called me, and of the debt of gratitude I should henceforth be asked to pay by striving to be a perfect Carmelite. I cannot describe what Holy Communion meant to me on that day.

After the Mass, our bishop put three questions to me to which I gave the prescribed answers with all the sincerity of my heart.

"What do you demand?"

"The mercy of God, the poverty of the Order, and the company of the sisters."

"Is it of your own free will and inclination that you desire to take the Habit of Religion?"

"Yes, your Excellency."

"Will you guard these things for the love of Our Lord alone?"

"Yes, with the grace of God and the prayers of the sisters."

As a sign of my "dying" to the world, I cut a piece of hair off and removed the jewelry I wore. Then, leaving the Choir, I went to exchange the bridal attire for the outer tunic (Habit) that the bishop had already blessed.

Returning to Choir, clothed in the brown tunic, linen toque, and small veil, I knelt before the Communion window. Our bishop touched each remaining piece of the holy Habit (cincture, Scapular, mantle) as our Mother passed an end of each through the Communion window. Then his Excellency recited the prayers about

which I already told you, as each successive part of the holy Habit was put on me. Clothed finally, with the help of our Mother, in the Habit for which I had so long yearned, I went to the center of the Choir.

There I lay flat on the floor with arms extended to form a cross — symbolic again of my death to the world. Prostrate during the chanting of the *Veni Creator*, I prayed earnestly for all my loved ones, for all priests, and for all those who had recommended themselves to our prayers. A little paper pinned over my heart had listed on it these many intentions. We believe that Jesus will grant every petition that His bride makes during the prostration; hence, I prayed for all — especially you. At the end of the prayers, I arose and received the crown of flowers.

Then, with the beautifully adorned candle in my hand, I knelt at the Communion window to receive the bishop's blessing. Before blessing me, however, his Excellency gave me my religious name: Sister Marie of the Trinity. My heart pounded with joy at the name! How like our Mother to let me keep my baptismal name because of my love for Mary; how wonderful to be dedicated, as our Blessed Mother was, to the Blessed Trinity!

You know how we spent the rest of the day: visiting in the grate room and meeting the many friends of Carmel who wished to greet the "new bride." May God reward you for all you did to make that day such a happy one. I have begun my canonical year of Novitiate — the time of very special grace.

This year "has for its object," as the *Constitutions* state, "the forming of the mind of the novice by the study of the holy *Rule* and *Constitutions*; by meditations and assiduous prayer; by learning what appertains to the vows and virtues; by exercises fitted for rooting out the germs of vice, controlling the emotions, and acquiring of virtues." Please pray very earnestly that I may truly be formed into a perfect Carmelite, Mother and Dad. Neither you nor I ever liked halfway measures in anything. Be assured of my prayers for all at home each day.

Your loving daughter,
Sister Marie of the Trinity, D.C.[41]

---

[41] Prior to Vatican II, these initials were used to designate "Discalced Carmelite." Presently, the initials O.C.D. are universally used in the Order. They stand for the official title of the Order in Latin: *Ordinis Carmelitarum Discalceatorum.*

Letter Twenty-Three

Dearest Mother, Dad, and all my loved ones,
Praised be Jesus Christ!

How it amused me when you wrote: "Why do you have days of retreat? Your whole life is like one long retreat!" Yes, you are right; our life does resemble a prolonged retreat, but nonetheless we *need* days of retreat. Somehow, we always have ourselves to contend with in this business of growing in sanctity. You know how much I studied to master the various subjects we learned at school. Well, I must study ever so much harder to attain to the stature of a genuine Carmelite.

Retreats, day of recollection, spiritual conferences, and sermons are the means afforded of studying this all-important subject. Our daily spiritual reading, which is made after Vespers each day, keeps us in touch with divine truths and acquaints us with the virtues we should acquire. The weekly conference particularizes on some cogent truth and makes us realize it a little better. Still, the monthly day of recollection, the annual retreat, and the private retreats that we may be permitted to make are special features whose value can hardly be estimated.

On these precious days, the silence is much more strict: we do not have any recreation; we avoid any kind of work that might necessitate questioning another sister. There are extra periods devoted to reading, four hours of meditation, and free time during which we may pray or just think. If there is a retreat master, his Reverence gives a conference at each of the four meditation periods.[42] The reading at meals is designed to carry on the theme of the retreat; hence, every moment of every hour recalls our minds most forcibly to the consideration of some prime truth.

When we first learned about the retreat schedule, some days before our annual retreat actually began, one postulant was wide-eyed as her Charity asked, "How can the poor priest talk at six o'clock in the morning?" I was thinking, "How will I ever understand anything at that hour?"

Carmelites must learn to pray well; for this is our vocation. Not that prayer is the end toward which we aim, but rather it is the indispensable means of attaining the end of our vocation—union with God. Our holy Mother, St. Teresa, simplified the complex nature of prayer by calling it a "friendly conversation with God." At the same time, this seraphic saint pointed out that humility is the foundation stone. Now you see, Mother and Dad, what deep lessons we must learn by dint of earnest day-by-day efforts—to know God as our best friend that we may more easily converse with Him and to acquire the solid virtue of humility. A whole lifetime is too short a time to learn these. Our retreats are so many shortcuts to the acquiring of this knowledge.

Our Carmelite Father pointed out what Carmel signifies in a very beautiful way. To his Reverence, the "C" is for charity: love

---

[42] In order to allow the nuns more time for quiet prayer and solitude, there are now only two conferences given each day. In addition, there is a Holy Hour with the Blessed Sacrament exposed, at which the Rosary is prayed and there is time for adoration.

Charity
Abnegation
Recollection
Mental Prayer
Edification
Love of
our Lady

of God and love of our neighbor—the basic element of Carmelite spirituality. "A" means abnegation, severing the ties that bind us to earth, to our self-love, our self-will, that we might be free to give ourselves wholly to God. "R": recollection is the means whereby we become one with God, walking in His holy presence and doing all solely for His honor and glory. "M": meditation or mental prayer is the expression we can give our love for God, the means through which we can attain to close union with Him. "E": edification is the help we give each other, the inspiration that our good acts exercise on our fellow religious for whose sanctification we are in a great measure responsible. "L" stands for Our Lady and bespeaks our love for Mary. Every Carmelite knows that the more she molds her life on the pattern of our Blessed Mother's, the more pleasing she will be to God. Then, too, there is no one more interested in helping us to attain to true sanctity than the wonderful Queen of Carmel.

This is a beautiful epitome of Carmel; yet it is a pointed reminder of what we must attain. Oh, we *do* need days set aside to consider these truths and the little progress we have thus far made. It is not just for our own sanctification that we strive for perfection but for all souls for whom we pray. Our father St. John of the Cross, the Doctor of Love, has summed up the reason for our efforts to attain to true love of God in a very beautiful sentence: "An instant of pure love is more precious in the sight of God and more profitable to the Church than all good works put together." It is our "apostolate," this sanctification of self, that we may truly be a powerhouse of prayer for others.

Do not wonder that I call Carmel a "powerhouse of prayer." If you could read the countless petitions we receive and the no-less-numerous letters of gratitude, the name would seem most apt. Each day we include all the intentions recommended to us as well as all our benefactors in the Divine Office, Mass, and all the other prayers and little sacrifices that fill our Carmelite life. Besides these offerings we have the perpetual novena in honor of the Infant Jesus of Prague; special prayers after supper (or collation); and the prayers in honor of the Seven Sorrows and Joys of our father St. Joseph each Sunday. All of these are especially offered for our benefactors and the intentions recommended to our prayers. There is a bulletin board just outside the Choir on which are posted the most urgent petitions. For these the sisters usually obtain permission to do special penances or to say extra prayers. Charity to all is, as you can see, the motivating force in Carmel, Mother and Dad, and our retreats help us to attain to this charity.

I hope you and Dad can make the Cana retreat, Mother. You will understand better after making one just how valuable a retreat can be! I know Dad will grumble a little bit about how we are trying to make a monk of him; but he will want to make the annual retreat part of his yearly schedule after he makes the first one. I guess you did not expect such a sermon as a result of your simple question, "Why a retreat?"—but I want to share every one of Carmel's benefits with you.

May God love and bless each one of you. Please keep praying for me as I always do for you.

Your loving daughter,
Sister Marie of the Trinity, D.C.

Monastery of the Holy Cross

THE DISCALCED CARMELITE COMMUNITY IN Iron Mountain, Michigan, Monastery of the Holy Cross, consisting of both cloistered and extern sisters, lives that simple family spirit and joyous austerity as cloistered contemplative religious with papal enclosure that St. Teresa wanted to reign in her Carmels.

Faithful to the Magisterium and to the beautiful traditions of their Order, they cherish that solitude and silence of their enclosure and consider it a privilege to wear the holy Habit of Our Lady. Daily life in their monastery reflects St. Teresa's wish to preserve the eremitical spirit of the early hermits on Mount Carmel within the loving and supportive setting of community life.

In loving submission to Holy Mother Church and in fidelity to their founding charism, they live out their spousal consecration to Jesus, their Beloved, through the offering of themselves for the salvation of souls and especially for priests.

Front view of the Monastery of the Holy Cross in Iron Mountain, Michigan

The crucifix shrine on the grounds of the monastery

The monastery grounds garden enclosure

The Our Lady of Lourdes Grotto

Sisters praying at the Our Lady of Lourdes Grotto

The Sacred Heart Shrine

The Our Lady of Mount Carmel Shrine

Letter Twenty-Four

$\mathcal{D}$ear Mother, Dad, and all my loved ones,

May the Queen of Carmel protect each one of you.

Your interesting letters about the vacation trip to St. Ann's shrine were very welcome, as were, also, the postal card pictures of that beautiful spot. Thanks be to God you had a happy and a safe trip.

We had some excitement last week — the election of the Reverend Mother Prioress. Our Mother, whom you met on my clothing day, was re-elected, as was, also, Mother Sub-Prioress. It was so very impressive when after the elections were over, the bell summoned all the sisters to the Choir. As you probably already guessed, only the final professed Choir nuns have a vote. But when the voting was finished, every one of the community went to the Choir. We all wore our white mantles as at other special functions. The grate curtain was open, so we had our faces veiled.[43]

---

[43] As noted elsewhere, the veils are no longer lowered over the face. The curtain is opened for the Holy Sacrifice of the Mass every day in order to allow the nuns to fully participate. However, the grate is so arranged as to guard the recollection and privacy of the nuns.

Then our good bishop, who had presided at the election, said the prayers that confirmed our Mother in office as Prioress of our Carmel for three years. After these prayers, we chanted the *Te Deum*, and then, one by one, beginning with the senior sisters, we knelt to kiss our Mother's Scapular and render our obedience.

On the Sunday after our Mother was elected, we had another election—this time for the Prior of our Carmel. Every sister, even the novices and postulants, were permitted to vote at this election for which we assembled, clad in our white mantles, in the Choir. Since the ballots all bore the name of the one sole candidate, our father St. Joseph, the election was unanimous. After the election, the *Te Deum* was chanted. Then the keys of the monastery were hung on the statue of the saint and the holy *Rule* placed before him. This act showed our confidence in his power to protect us from external evils as well as to guide us in the observance to which we are bound. Our Mother then carried the statue through the monastery while we, chanting the beautiful liturgical hymns in his honor, accompanied her Reverence.

This silent saint is a worthy model for our contemplative life. If only we could acquire his deep love of and confidence in God, we should be perfect Carmelites. The intimacy with Jesus and Mary, which was not only his privilege but also the source of his wonderful sanctity, is the goal of our hours of prayer and recollection.

Would you like to hear a little bit about our devotion to this oft-forgotten saint and how it began? It will no doubt surprise you as much as it did me to learn that it really was the Order of Carmel that spread devotion to the father of Jesus. The great Pope Benedict XIV wrote: "The Carmelites brought the public cult of St. Joseph from the East when they emigrated to the West." Our holy Order, therefore, had the wonderful privilege of erecting the first church in Europe ever dedicated to the honor of this great saint. Even the feast in his honor was celebrated in Carmel long before it was extended to the universal Church. This was but the natural outcome, though, of Carmel's whole purpose, which St. Mary Magdalen de Pazzi summed up in this exclamation: "Joseph, united as he is to Jesus and Mary, is like a bright shining star that protects those souls who fight the battle of life under Mary's standard (the Scapular of Carmel)."

Devotion to St. Joseph had been a part of Carmelite tradition from the very first days of our holy Order; but a new impetus was given to this already fervent devotion when, on several occasions, our dear Lord and our Blessed Mother spoke of it to the holy reformer of Carmel, our holy Mother, St. Teresa. Our holy Mother relates the incidents in her *Life*:

> One day after Holy Communion, the Lord gave me the most explicit commands to work for this aim (the foundation of the reformed Carmel) and made me wonderful promises.... It should be called St. Joseph's.... St. Joseph would watch over us at one door and Our Lady at the other, and He (Christ) would be with us....
>
> At this same period ... I thought Our Lady took me by the hands and told me that I was giving her great pleasure by serving the glorious St. Joseph, and that I might be sure that all I was trying to do about the convent would be accomplished.

You can imagine with what joy we Carmelites carry on the tradition thus established by our holy Mother. We never refer to him as St. Joseph but rather as our glorious father or our holy father St. Joseph. We have shrines in his honor throughout the monastery and celebrate his several feasts with special joy. Just as you depend on Dad for the necessaries at home, Mother, we depend on our holy father St. Joseph for the needed things in our Carmel.

To remind him of whatever might be needed, we have a little altar in his honor in the provisory (Carmelite pantry), where we keep a vigil light burning and vases of flowers when these are available. Before his statue, enshrined there, we place the last of whatever article is running short. For example, one day we had just one egg left. As you can well understand, eggs appear on the Carmelite menu quite often to take the place of meat. Sister said a little prayer to our good provider and placed the one remaining egg on the bracket to remind him of our need. Within a few days, he inspired some very generous benefactors to bring us a whole case of eggs. That is the way it happens every time.

You, too, can participate in our devotion to this wonderful saint. By wearing the Scapular, you are the special children of Mary and therefore the special children of her spouse. His care will far surpass your most ardent desires. Just listen to what our holy Mother, St. Teresa, says in her *Life*: "God has granted to other saints only the grace to help in this or that particular need, but I know from experience that the glorious St. Joseph extends his power to all our necessities."

Let us frequently pray to our father St. Joseph for our needs as well as the needs of the whole Church. God love and bless all of you.

Your loving daughter,
Sister Marie of the Trinity, D.C.

Letter Twenty-Five

*D*ear Mother, Dad, and all,
      Praised be Jesus Christ!
You are wondering about "my room": How it is furnished? If it
is large and bright? If it is warm enough? Your parental love inspires
these loving queries, so I do want to relieve you of all anxiety.

The first thing is to tell you that we never say "my room." In
fact, we never say "my" for anything. Everything—our clothing,
books, and whatever else we use—is common property; hence, we
always refer to them as *our* Habit or *our* books. The word "room"
is replaced by "cell," so instead of *my* room, I shall describe "*our*
cell." The word "cell" has nothing of a prison connotation, unless
we wish to regard ourselves as "prisoners of Love." It is the ancient
term used to designate the sleeping rooms, which term has been
in use among religious for many centuries.

Now to describe our cell. It is quite small, measuring about six
by eight feet. As this is a remodeled old dwelling, the ceilings are
quite high. It is bright because each cell has at least one window.[44]

---

[44] The descriptions here refer to the original provisional monastery.
The current monastery, built in 1965, has cells of more adequate

The myth that Carmelites live in drab, dark, gloomy houses is certainly not true. There is very little furniture in the cell—but everything necessary *is* there.

The bed, a plank placed on two trestles, is on one side. Its mattress is thin, but that does not bother us. We have sufficient blankets to keep us warm during these northern nights. The woolen sheets and a woolen pillowcase seemed scratchy at first; but after a few weeks, they did not bother me either. The spread is of brown wool, as is also the pillow coverlet. A wooden cross, about twelve inches long, rests on the pillow in the day, which cross we hold during the night; but it is no hindrance to sound sleep.

Beside the bed is a small stool. The only other furniture in the cell is a small stand in which we keep our necessaries, such as toothbrush, handkerchief, basin, and soap. We fill our wash basin each evening for use in the morning. As I told you before, the cold water is a good awakener.[45]

There is a large wooden cross hanging behind the bed, on which there is no "corpus" since we are to be crucified with our dear Lord. We have a picture, inexpensive but devotional, on the wall. Our holy Mother, St. Teresa, wanted to see a holy picture whatever way her Reverence turned; so our Mother has supplied us with this help. It really does keep one's mind on spiritual things if one can see reminders of our dear Lord, His Blessed Mother, and the saints.

We try to stay in our cell whenever we are not employed in some special office of the monastery, since hand sewing, reading,

---

dimensions and with windows looking out upon our rural, wooded property.

[45] Sinks were included in each cell in the "new" monastery at the insistence of Bishop Thomas Noa.

and writing can be done in this secluded and much-loved spot. As occasion arises, we may ask permission to take a small worktable to our cell to facilitate our work. We find God in this little room: stripped as it is of worldly adornments, it makes us think of our Creator. Our windows are frosted glass so that we cannot see things beyond the enclosure;[46] but the upper pane is clear, through which we can see only the beautiful sky, the tall trees, the snow and rain. All this helps us in our quest for God.

Every Carmelite loves the cell assigned to her. Oh, yes, it is assigned; we do not choose. Nor can we become attached to it; for changes are made without forewarning. These changes sometimes cause amusing incidents. One sister arose to make a Holy Hour one night, which just happened to be the first night in her "new" cell. As her Charity came back rather drowsily at about 1:00 a.m.,

---

[46] This precaution is no longer necessary. The windows look out over the wooded property within the enclosure, and the trees screen any views from beyond.

it completely slipped her mind about the change of cells. So – into her former cell Sister quietly walked. As her Charity started to retire, the sister in bed stirred! At first, Sister was surprised – then she remembered! "Oh, this is not our cell," her Charity gasped, as she quickly stepped into the corridor.

Whichever cell is ours pleases us. Maybe there is cause for a wee bit of self-denial if we are next to a sister who, because of severe headaches, finds the least noise a trial; but how many souls can be saved by our efforts to be quiet. Or maybe the snoring of a neighbor makes us lose some sleep. Again, offered in union with our dear Lord's pain, this tiny suffering acquires great value. Each moment gives us the metal of which we can make coins to purchase souls. God grant that we may never waste any opportunity. To show our unworthiness even to dwell in this "garden of Christ," our Carmel, we kneel to kiss the floor each time we enter our cell, and again before we leave it. This little custom expresses our appreciation to God for calling us here.

During the past week, I spent some extra time in our much-loved little cell. A rather severe throat infection was the cause of my having to stay in bed several days. It is all cleared up now, Mother, so do not worry. And do not worry that the bed is too hard for a sick person. When the illness is not serious nor of long duration, we remain in our cell; but if a sister is really seriously ill, or if one should have an ailment requiring a long period in bed, the infirmary is used.

The infirmary is a bright room situated on the second floor near the front of the monastery so that it can be easily reached by the priest if the sacraments are to be administered. In it, besides a real hospital bed with springs and mattress, is a lovely little altar. What a joy it must be for an ill sister to see our dear Lord come to this altar so that she can receive Holy Communion.

Now, you see, Mother and Dad, everything is well arranged in our little Carmel. Do not worry about your Carmelite; only join with her in thanking the good God for the wonderful grace of a Carmelite vocation. You and all my loved ones share in my daily prayers.

Your loving daughter,
Sister Marie of the Trinity, D.C.

Letter Twenty-Six

*D*earest Mother, Dad, and all,
    May Christ's presence fill your souls with peace.

After describing our cell to you in the last letter, it seems only right to tell you now about the Novitiate. This is "home" for us during our first years in Carmel. Here we spend most of our time and learn the precious lessons that should make us true Carmelites.

According to canon law, the novices (and postulants) are to have no intercourse with professed sisters.[47] Hence, the part of the monastery reserved for the novices is, as far as possible, set off from the rest of the house. In our little Carmel, since it is really a remodeled dwelling, the Novitiate is a combination oratory, workroom, and recreation room.

At that end of the room that is set apart for the oratory, there is an altar. Beneath the *mensa* of this altar is built a glass-enclosed niche. Through the glass we see a manger in which rests the most beautiful statue of the Infant Jesus — so lifelike that one must look

[47] Canon law has since been revised in 1983. This particular norm no longer exists. There is still a certain separation, yet with greater interaction between the novices and the rest of the community.

twice to convince herself it is not real. This is the Model on whom the novices are to mold their lives; for the humility, simplicity, and obedience of the Infant Jesus are the virtues we should acquire.

A statue of our Blessed Mother and one of our father St. Joseph are placed at the side of the altar, while behind it hangs a beautiful Crucifix. We rearrange and decorate this altar according to the liturgical seasons and the particular feasts.

At the back of the room, in the work and recreation part, are our tables and sewing machines. We have much use for these, since it is our duty to wash and mend the community clothes. Thus we learn the basic things about sewing and are, little by little, prepared to help with the more intricate sewing of vestments, Infant Jesus outfits, and altar linens.

Some of the sisters know how to sew when they enter, which is a real help for the community. Since this is one of the main works of Carmel, it is necessary for those to learn after entering who do not know how to sew before their entrance. I am more grateful each day, Mother dear, for all you taught Sis and me. I know it was quite a task for you to convince us that we should spend some time during our summer vacation learning how to crochet, to embroider, and to mend the family clothes. The tennis court or the bicycle was always more inviting than the sewing basket. But I can assure Sis that she will never regret learning how to sew—whatever state of life she may embrace.

Now that you know how the room looks, I shall tell you about our life in the Novitiate. Morning prayers are said, in common, by the novices about fifteen minutes after the alarm. The morning offering is followed by prayers to our dear Lord, our Blessed Mother, our guardian angel, our father St. Joseph, and the patron saints of our holy Order. Then the sister appointed reads the intentions of the day: for example, Sunday is offered in union with all the angels and saints who forever praise the Adorable Trinity; as an act of reparation for blasphemy; and for our Holy Father, Pope Pius XII,[48] and the needs of the Church. This inspiring practice helps us to keep our thoughts on God and our every action directed to His glory. After breakfast we are again summoned to the Novitiate. The Litany of the Blessed Virgin Mary is followed by a special prayer that invokes Mary's blessing on each action of the day. Then our Novice Mistress gives us the blessing. We next sit back on our heels on the floor to listen to the spiritual reading and instruction. (Sitting on the floor is a special act of mortification performed by the novices whenever they are in the Novitiate.[49])

The reading usually begins with a chapter of the *Constitutions* or *Ceremonial* of our holy Order. We may put questions to our Mother Mistress concerning these points of observance and decorum. Then our Mother Mistress reads a little from some spiritual book, such as *The Carmelite Directory of the Spiritual Life*, the *Cistercian Spiritual Directory for Religious*, or *Christian Perfection* by St. Alphonsus Rodriguez. After this, our Mother Mistress instructs us how we can put into practice in our own lives the virtues described.[50] Life in Carmel is so simple; yet we can find so many things to make us holy. Little things, oh yes, but the precious gold with which we can purchase souls.

Sometimes our Mother Mistress just talks to us — pointing out ways in which we have failed to act as good religious and exhorting us to strive faithfully to do better. An unguarded look, a noisy

[48] The nuns always keep in prayer the Supreme Pontiff currently reigning.

[49] Simple wooden stools are now used. The custom of sitting on the floor during the times of prayer is optional.

[50] The Iron Mountain Carmel now has a formation plan approved by the Holy See.

action, or an overeager question betrays a lack of the real religious spirit. Excusing or defending ourselves for actions that are faulty is considered a real failure. Our holy Mother, St. Teresa, was very emphatic when she denounced this form of pride. These are the negative points.

Being cheerful even when we feel ill, going on when we are very tired, never complaining about any inconvenience are some very positive helps to sanctity. Religious life is, as the Little Flower so well described it, "a martyrdom of pin-pricks." There is an abiding peace, however, that makes the rough way easy to trod. When you hear about our recreations together in the Novitiate, you will understand better how sweet it is to dwell in Carmel.

Until I can write again, may God be with you and Mary protect you.

Your loving daughter,
Sister Marie of the Trinity, D.C.

Letter Twenty-Seven

*D*ear Mother, Dad, and all,
  Praised be Jesus Christ!

"Don't you get tired living with the same people all the time?" This was a question put to me recently in one of my friend's letters. Since you might be worrying that this misfortune will happen to your daughter, I want to tell you why we never tire of living with the same sisters, Mother and Dad.

As cloistered nuns, Carmelites usually spend their whole religious life in the same monastery, where there are not more than twenty-one nuns. This living with such a small group over a period of years might be a very great trial; for, after all, we do remain human in the cloister. We each have our individual personality, character traits, and disposition. Our saintly founders, having foreseen the dangers of our secluded life, have made many and very wise rules and regulations that help to avert friction and maintain the wonderful "family spirit" so peculiar to Carmel.

"Our Mother" is the loving name by which we address our Prioress. To the sisters, we always say "your Charity" instead of simply "you" or "her Charity" instead of "her." This connotes the love that we feel for those who, like ourselves, are called to be the spouses of Christ. If, in conversation, we refer to our Mother, we use the term "her Reverence," thus indicating the superior position that the office gives.

It is a constant reminder of home when I observe the many little courtesies here in our Carmelite family. As we children saw our dear parents treat our grandmothers with such respect, we learned to treat Mother and Dad with that same loving respect. So, too, here in Carmel—we younger sisters observe how our senior sisters treat our Mother with respect and each other with courtesy. We thus imitate what we see and we, too, treat our Mother with marks of special respect and veneration.

All rise when her Reverence enters a room, even the Choir or refectory. If one of the novices meets our Mother in the corridors during the day, her Charity kneels with folded hands to kiss her Reverence's Scapular. As you know, it is an indulgenced act to kiss any Brown Scapular of our Blessed Lady of Mount Carmel; hence, to kiss our Mother's is not only an act of reverence toward authority but also a means of helping the suffering souls in Purgatory.[51]

I hope you still carry on that beautiful custom we observed each night when I was at home—that of whispering, "Good night and God bless you," as we went off to bed. Here in Carmel, before retiring each night, we have a somewhat similar custom. Each sister kneels at her cell door until our Mother comes to give the blessing. Her Reverence uses the beautiful night prayer of the Church while making the Sign of the Cross over each of her "spiritual daughters": "*Noctem quietum* ... May the Lord Almighty grant you a quiet night and perfect end."

---

[51] Some of these customs have been changed over the years, but the spirit behind them remains the same.

In the Choir and refectory, there are other little marks of mutual courtesy that keep alive the spirit of fraternal love. Should a sister arrive late in either of these places, on reaching her place, her Charity makes a slight inclination of the head to each of the sisters who are beside her. The same is done before leaving one's place if a sister is obliged to leave earlier than the others. One sister had a beautiful interpretation of this little custom: "I like to think that I am saluting Jesus within the soul of my companion when I incline my head." It is just this—seeing Jesus in the souls of our companions—that makes community life so inspiring. You see, since we observe silence in these places, the inclination of the head takes the place of the loving greeting or farewell uttered in the family circle.

Of course, as with everything new, I have blundered in these acts of courtesy. How many times I knelt to kiss our Mother's Scapular and found, to my embarrassment, that I had mistaken one of the professed nuns for her Reverence. Usually the poor sister I thus accosted was more embarrassed even than I.

During my first week in Carmel, my companion at the table always sat down late because her Charity was pouring the beverage. Her Charity's inclination of the head to me was not returned! I thought that Sister was looking at our dish to see if I had been served everything; so I leaned over each time to whisper, "I have plenty, thank you, Sister." There I was—breaking the rule of silence and probably causing poor Sister much distraction—but ignorance is a valid excuse for many things.

In the Choir, too, when the sister beside me came back from ringing the bell, I thought her inclination of the head was an effort to see our breviary in order to find the place. "It's funny that Sister looks at our book for the place," I thought. "Surely her Charity must know that I am almost always mixed up about the place—but

ECCE QUAM BONUM

I better show her Charity." So I pushed our breviary over in front of Sister. Now I really marvel at the wonderful charity the sisters showed when they did not laugh at my many foolish blunders. That is the spirit of sisterly love that makes our life so happy.

We may, with permission, visit sick sisters to encourage and console them. While being careful never to interfere with the assigned duties of each sister, we may do little acts of charity such as carry heavy articles to lighten their work. Our silence during most of the day is another help to mutual love. It eliminates gossiping and backbiting criticism that are such peace destroyers.

"*Ecce quam bonum* ... Behold, how good and how pleasant it is for brethren to dwell together in unity." These are the words of Psalm 132, which we chant as we embrace each other on certain festive occasions. How true it is; how wonderful it is to live in harmony with those who love what we love—God, who is Love. I think that psalm could be your theme song at home too; so I asked our Mother's permission to copy it on a little piece of parchment for you. The printing is not so good.

My daily prayer is that the good God continue to bless you with His best gifts and graces.

Your loving daughter,
Sister Marie of the Trinity, D.C.

Letter Twenty-Eight

*D*ear Mother, Dad, and all my loved ones,
    Praised be Jesus Christ!
I think it was the saintly Benedictine Abbot Marmion who said that "joy is the echo of God's presence within us." The quotation may not be exact; but its meaning is a good description of recreation here in Carmel. Only God's wonderful presence could give such joy!

As you already know, there are two hours of recreation each day: one after the midday meal and the other immediately following the evening collation or supper. We finish the dishes as quickly as possible, and then the professed sisters go to the community room while the novices assemble in the Novitiate for an hour of wholesome relaxation. We are forbidden to play any games such as cards, checkers, or ball. Instead, we do some kind of handwork such as sewing or embroidering while we chat together. The professed sisters may speak with each other, but the novices must direct their conversation to the Mother Mistress. This wise regulation helps to ward off anything like worldliness or too much intimacy in the conversation of young sisters who are just being trained to religious modes of speaking.[52]

How we enjoy hearing of funny accidents that one or another of us has had! How much good-natured bantering there is about our foolish mistakes! We share with each other, too, the delight we find in some particularly interesting book, or we listen eagerly as our Mother Mistress relates stories about the early days of our little Carmel. We can profit from the instructions concerning sewing or other work that is given to one in particular. Often others have the same difficulties as we — and that is some sort of consolation for our ignorance.

One of the funniest things happened last summer. It was a great feast, so we were recreating with the professed sisters. As the day was so warm, we had gone out to spend the recreation on our veranda at the end of the garden. There were a few clouds in the sky, but no one except Mother Sub-Prioress really thought that it would rain. Her Reverence, however, deemed it prudent to take our only umbrella out with her.

Well it turned out that Mother Sub-Prioress was right. A storm broke so suddenly that we could not get to the house. We were safe enough; but the storm was a long one. Finally, our Mother said that we would just have to go because it was late. We had one umbrella for the whole community — and Mother Sub-Prioress had somewhat of a priority on its use.

Then someone had an idea. "Why not hold our stools over our heads as we run to the door?" No sooner suggested than done. We must have made quite a sight. The funniest sight, however, was

---

[52] The novices are allowed greater freedom to speak with one another during recreation and need not direct their speech through the Novice Mistress.

Mother Sub-Prioress and the two sisters who tried to share her umbrella. Her Reverence is tall and takes short quick steps: the other two sisters were small and had to run like chickens to keep up with her Reverence.

That was an accidental entertainment; but sometimes there are planned events that give us real fun. I do not think you ever heard about what happened last All Saints' Day. Since that, too, is a great feast, the novices were recreating with the professed in the community room. The next day being All Souls' Day, the conversation naturally turned to the Poor Souls. Stories were related about the devotion of certain saints who prayed especially for the Suffering Souls, and how these saints were frequently visited by the souls for whom they prayed, during which visits the Poor Souls revealed the reasons for their purgation and the number of years their sufferings must last. One story followed another until all of us were on the edge of our stools.

All of a sudden, the lights went out! While Mother Sub-Prioress was nervously fumbling in the dark to find the stub of a candle, her Reverence was encouraging the rest of us, saying, "Now don't be frightened, our Mother! Don't worry, Sisters! It's only a fuse. I'm sure it's only a fuse."

Then came the excitement! We saw a light floating through the air, and it was coming right toward the room where we were seated. As the light came closer, we could distinguish bright, burning eyes and a big toothless grin. Under the head was a long, flowing white figure. Then everyone laughed. It was only a pumpkin head, and beneath the flowing gown (sheet) was the sister who had kitchen duty that week.

Then we knew why our Mother just sat quietly and waited when the lights went out. Her Reverence had given Sister permission to play the prank. In fact, her Reverence had even helped with it by turning out the lights!

In the warm months, the professed sisters as well as the novices spend recreations taking care of the garden and yard. The small plot set aside for the vegetables is usually so full of plants that we can hardly make our way through in order to weed it; but it is the best we can do until we have more property.[53]

When our good benefactors send us bushels of tomatoes, apples, or other fruits, we spend our recreations peeling and canning so that the food bills can be kept low during the winter months. Sometimes we have general housecleaning recreations. These hours of hard work are nonetheless refreshing since we recreate together and make fun of the otherwise burdensome work.

On great feast days, as mentioned above, the novices are permitted to go to the community room to recreate with the professed sisters.[54] On these occasions, we novices are allowed to speak directly with each other. These occasions are that much more happy because they are so rare.

Each Friday we spend one period of recreation with the professed sisters, during which we have a discussion on spiritual matters.[55] How much better I understand the *Catechism* from these informal discussions about the fundamental truths of our religion. I was rather worried the first time as to whether it would be a

---

[53] The present property of twenty-one acres has plenty of room for two large vegetable gardens, apple orchards, shrines with flower beds besides the fields, and woods allowing for a prayerful setting and healthy exercise.

[54] According to new regulations, the novices come to all recreations with the professed nuns, in accord with the spirit of St. Teresa.

[55] The custom described here was not of long duration in the Iron Mountain Carmel. Such discussions may arise spontaneously at any recreation or may be more formally held at a Chapter meeting.

question-answer testing of my *Catechism* knowledge. It turned out to be a very enlightening discussion.

At the beginning of each month, we spend an hour of recreation with the professed in order to draw our patron saint for the month. The little card bearing the saint's name also tells us the special virtue we should practice during that month. We have a similar drawing on New Year's Day, at which we receive our patron saints for the year and learn which virtues we should especially strive to acquire.

At that same recreation, we also draw the names of the diocesan priests for whom we are to pray during the ensuing year. Each priest and seminarian of our diocese has a sister especially appointed to pray for his needs and intentions. Another interesting raffle is held at which we draw one of the seven sacraments of the Church. Then we pray for those who receive that particular sacrament so that they may be worthy recipients and may gain all the graces attached to its reception. All these practices are so many incentives to fervent prayer—so many interesting events in our simple but joyous life.

Without any special raffle at which I could draw your names, I keep you in my daily prayers. Please pray for your Carmelite always. May Jesus keep you and Mary ever guard you.

Your loving daughter,
Sister Marie of the Trinity, D.C.

Letter Twenty-Nine

Dear Mother, Dad, and all my loved ones,
    May Jesus live in your souls!

Your questions are sometimes beyond my very limited knowledge. The recent one, "Where is the Mother General of Carmelites?" sent me hurrying to our Mother Mistress for enlightenment. Vaguely I was aware that our community was independent of every other Carmel; but what that might mean just never dawned on me. Now, with my recently acquired knowledge, I can answer your question and at the same time tell you about the beginning of Carmel of the Holy Cross.

To begin with, each Carmel is autonomous. That is, each one is distinct from every other as far as government is concerned. Each has its own Novitiate, and each maintains itself by its own work and resources. There is a bond, however, in the fact that all Discalced Carmelites follow the same holy *Rule* and *Constitutions*. All, too, follow the same *Ceremonial*—the book that gives detailed explanations as to how we should conduct ourselves in Choir, in the refectory, and at all other times. The bonds of fraternal interest and mutual prayers draw our Carmels together into one large family; but since Carmelite Prioresses rank as major superiors, there is no Mother General. Has this clarified your problem?

If so, I am sure that now a new question is posed in your minds: "Where and how do Carmels come into being?" A new Carmel is founded when a bishop requests that an established Carmel send subjects to his diocese. The Holy See must give the final approval to the foundation. Then, once founded, this new Carmel is independent of the Mother Carmel that the original group of sisters left.

Carmels in the United States can trace their origins back to France, Belgium, and Mexico. During the terrible persecutions in Mexico when religious men and women were forced to leave their convents and to seek refuge in secret places, several Carmelite Nuns managed to cross the border into the United States. These, after weary months of seeking a home, were welcomed into the Grand Rapids diocese by his Excellency Bishop Richter and founded there the Carmel of Our Lady of Guadalupe.

Destitute and foreign, these heroic women placed entire confidence in our father St. Joseph. How richly this trust was repaid by that wonderful saint, who inspired leading Catholic laypersons to help the little community. Several more refugee sisters soon joined the little group. God showered graces on the work, and gradually, as the Carmel became better known, American girls entered the cloister. Five Carmels were founded from this ever-fruitful Mother Carmel — our Carmel of the Holy Cross here in Iron Mountain being the latest.

The sisters destined to begin the work here left Grand Rapids on the feast of the Presentation of the Blessed Mother, November 21, 1950. They rejoice to tell of the warm reception given them by his Excellency Bishop Noa, Monsignor Pelissier, and all the priests, religious, and lay people of this little city. It was Thanksgiving Day when the first Mass was offered in the little improvised chapel and the Blessed Sacrament reserved. Jesus had come to dwell with them—what joy that was!

The remodeling continued until the frame dwelling was a real little monastery. Our recent remodeling to enlarge several rooms gave all of us younger sisters a taste of what the first sisters endured. Dodging men during the day and using their tools during evening recreation—this is what remodeling in Carmel means. Dad will be pleasantly surprised to hear how his Carmelite knocked down old plaster and then put up lath when the new partitions were ready.

Sometimes, in the early days, it was hard to explain to the carpenters the needs of a monastery. The "turn" (a revolving shelf through which messages are received and packages passed in and out of the cloister) was one of these problems. Since no amount of verbal description gave a clear picture, our Mother resorted to making a small cardboard model. "Oh," said the astonished workmen, "you want a merry-go-round built in this wall! Well, we can do that easily enough." Then the work progressed quickly.

When our Carmel was founded, the sisters brought not only the holy *Rule*, *Constitutions*, and *Ceremonial* but some particular customs. As you will easily understand, little customs vary between one Carmel and another. This can probably best be explained by the realization that our strict enclosure makes intercourse impossible except by letter—and everyone knows how impossible it is to put everything in letters. So we have inherited from our Mother Carmel customs among which one of the most beautiful is a special devotion to the holy angels.

One of the very ancient Carmels in Mexico was situated in a dangerous position. The religious, in a deep spirit of faith, prayed daily to the three archangels and to the guardian angels to protect them and their monastery. One day, several evil-looking men knocked at the monastery door and requested to see the superior, who graciously received them as a safeguard against trouble or danger to the Carmel. The men very bluntly put their question: "Who, Sister, are those four young men who guard your monastery wall every night? We have made several attempts to rob your monastery; but as soon as we approach within its precincts, these four young men with swords in their hands appear on guard. We have always fled in terror, for there was something majestic in their bearing." The sisters could attribute this wonderful protection to no one save the angels to whom they had daily prayed and whose protection they had invoked. By degrees, other Carmels established this custom—the religious coming from Mexico bringing it with them to the United States and passing it on to the Carmels subsequently founded.

Each day, after the noon recreation, we have the visit to the most Blessed Sacrament in common. After the prescribed six Our Fathers, Hail Marys, and Glory Be's, the prayer in honor of the Blessed Sacrament is recited.

Then we have the commemorations in honor of the holy angels: "St. Michael, glorious prince, be mindful of us ...; St. Gabriel, angel of the Annunciation, help us to adore the Incarnate Son of God ...; St. Raphael, medicine of God, heal our wounds and guide us daily along the path of salvation ...; all you holy angels, guard and defend us in the daily struggle." Each beautiful antiphon, verse, and prayer is taken from the Divine Office composed to honor the respective angel. We are convinced that the blessed spirits are pleased with these acts of homage, and that they do really guard our Carmel.

When you come to visit our Carmel again, you will have a pleasant surprise. A very generous family, hearing of our devotion to the four angels, offered to give us a statue of each one. The statues are most beautiful. They will be placed on cement pedestals at each corner of our enclosure wall.[56]

I know that you always begin the day with that lovely prayer: "Angel of God, my guardian dear ..."; but I think you would find additional peace and joy in frequently calling on the other angels too. You will continue to have the special place in my prayers that you always have had. May our dear Lord and His wonderful Mother love you, and may the holy angels protect you.

Your loving daughter,
Sister Marie of the Trinity, D.C.

---

[56] The four statues mentioned here were brought to the new monastery. They stand on pedestals on the four corners of our private cemetery within the enclosure.

Letter Thirty

$\mathcal{D}$earest Mother, Dad, and all,
   May Jesus dwell in your hearts always!
How I enjoyed reading your letters. The news Sis sent was more than surprising. When I read that Patsy was really anxious to know about the requirements for entering Carmel, I just smiled. Patsy—the last one in the world that I ever dreamed would think of being a religious—actually seems to be thinking seriously about the matter. It was just like her to seek the information from Sis—just to keep me in the dark. Well, I shall be praying very much for her.

When I told our Mother Mistress about the questions Sis wanted answered, her Reverence very graciously helped me. I told her Reverence what kind of cut-up Patsy always was, and how it surprised me to know she was really considering the possibility of a religious vocation. "Oh, we find that type makes the best material to work with," was her Reverence's reply. Then she added, "From things I have heard, you were just about the same as your friend—so you really should not be so surprised."

As you must remember, Mother and Dad, many papers are required along with the application to enter Carmel. Baptismal, Confirmation, and health certificates must accompany the letters of recommendation. These are submitted to the Chapter (voting body of the community composed of final professed sisters). If the Chapter approves of the information submitted, the applicant may enter Carmel to begin her postulancy.[57]

The postulancy lasts at least six months for those aspiring to be Choir nuns and one year for the lay-sisters. During this period, the postulant wears the simple black dress that I have already described; takes part in all the exercises of prayer and penance; and is bound to keep the strict enclosure. It is a time of learning, during which she makes up her mind whether or not she really wants to be a Carmelite. We contract no obligation to stay when we enter. Rather, we are given ample opportunity of making our own decision, and we are free to go at any time. In fact, many do go either because they realize that such a life is not what they want, or else that it is simply beyond their strength.

At the end of the six months or year of probation, the Chapter decides whether or not the postulant shows evident signs of becoming a good Carmelite. If the professed sisters find the postulant worthy, then she may receive the holy Habit. The day on which the sister receives the holy Habit is the first of the canonical year of Novitiate. This is a year especially set aside to train the young novice in the ways and meanings of the religious life: what the vows are and what obligations they impose; what the "spirit of Carmel" is; and how one must strive to acquire that spirit of prayer and renunciation.

---

[57] The process of applying for entrance and the various stages of formation have been most recently updated by the document *Cor Orans* (2018). An aspirancy is now required, comprising at least one year of contact with the monastery before entering. Postulancy must be one year for all candidates and the Novitiate is two years.

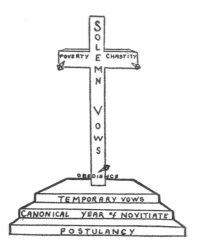

The year of Novitiate finished, the novice expresses her desire to pronounce her vows; and, if the professed sisters find her worthy, the profession of simple temporary vows binding for three years takes place.[58] "Temporary vows" — yes, Holy Mother Church wants this step to safeguard both the individual and the religious community. "Temporary" — but in the heart of the fervent novice is the firm conviction that at the end of the three-year trial period, these vows will be made binding *until death*.

The young professed remains in the Novitiate for two more years so that further training will enable her to become a more perfect Carmelite. However, the last year of the three years is spent with the professed sisters. This "leaving the Novitiate" is a real trial. The sisters whom I have seen go have seemed quite as homesick as I was when I entered, but it is a good plan. It enables the young sister to learn what professed life will be and also helps the professed sisters to become more thoroughly acquainted with her Charity.

---

[58] Five years of temporary vows are required now by the recent document *Cor Orans*.

Inside the Cloistered Life

The day on which the temporary vows expire, the sister is perfectly free to go; but if her Charity decides to persevere, there are the very moving ceremonies of solemn profession and the pontifical consecration. You will have to witness this latter ceremony to know why I yearn for that day to dawn in my life.

After giving me these points, our Mother Mistress laughed and said, "Maybe Patsy will be a really extraordinary religious." Her Reverence went on to tell me the story of a postulant who, during her first week in Carmel, sat down in the Prioress's place in the Choir to pray. "How soon," the older Mothers thought, "she aspires to be a superior!" Years later, that postulant did become a holy superior and was often reminded of this incident that seemed a prophecy of the future. That sounds like something Patsy might do!

Time to go. Please beg our dear Lord and His own wonderful Mother to make me worthy to take each step; to make me faithful to every grace of my Carmelite vocation; to give me the stamina I need so that someday I may be consecrated His spouse. Your prayers will obtain for me the graces I need. You always share in my prayers in a very special way.

Your loving daughter,
Sister Marie of the Trinity, D.C.

Letter Thirty-One

*D*earest Mother, Dad, and all my loved ones,
    Praised be Jesus Christ!

Neither the miles that separate us nor the walls that make me His prisoner can thwart your loving solicitude for my well-being. How like you, Mother dear, to be anxious about the examination of my eyes — but do not worry. Our dear Lord has promised those who leave all to follow Him that they will receive the hundredfold, and Carmel is no exception to that promise.

The doctors here are so kind and generous that they come to Carmel, since we cannot (except for surgery or other very grave reasons) go out to them.[59] Yes, the rule of enclosure, even papal enclosure, permits that doctors and needed workmen may enter to do their work. There are certain precautionary rules governing such entrances.

Each year the bishop must approve of the list of men that our Mother submits as being possibly needed. This list includes the names of doctors, dentists, carpenters, electricians, plumbers — all

[59] The new laws for papal enclosure do allow for leaving the cloister for doctor appointments.

men of good repute, though not necessarily Catholic. Then, when occasion arises that some secular person must enter the enclosure, our Mother is informed, and her Reverence gives the enclosure keys to the two professed sisters whose duty it is to accompany the seculars. These sisters wear the black veil down over their faces—a source of shock and sometimes discomfort to the visitor. Usually, however, the original misgivings melt away when the stranger hears the friendly voices from behind the veils.

One time a doctor came. To relieve his shock about the veiled face, Sister began to explain that it is part of our holy *Rule* since we have solemn vows. Finally, after the brief explanation, her Charity added, "But, of course, the one whose eyes are to be examined does not have her face veiled!" A loud chuckle of relief was followed by, "Well, that makes things better! I was just wondering how we would proceed with the eye examination under such hazards!"

You see, there is nothing to worry about. The eye doctor is so kind: he donated an electric eye chart, and he makes nothing of the inconvenience and trouble it causes him to bring all the other equipment to the monastery. Our dentists take turns coming so that each sister has her teeth cared for at least once a year. We have a little dental room furnished by one of the sisters' relatives and a generous dental supply house.[60] The Alleluia antiphon in the votive Mass of our Blessed Lady of Mount Carmel well expresses the truth: "Nothing was wanting to them while they were with us in Carmel. Alleluia." Surely our dear Lord and our wonderful father and provider, St. Joseph, inspire everyone to help us so that we lack nothing!

Does it surprise you about the veiled faces when we are with seculars? Lest you may imagine that this applies to our families,

---

[60] Since the sisters now go out to the dentist's office, the old equipment was donated to the missions.

I shall explain further. We are permitted to see our immediate family, mother, father, brothers, and sisters, without veiling our faces, just as I saw you on my "clothing day." Visits are always in the "grate room"; that is, we *never* leave the enclosure to visit in the outer parlor. You will, undoubtedly, always find this somewhat of a trial, but the strangeness will wear off little by little. It is part of our sacrifice for Him not to have the consolation of embracing our loved ones.

With others who may come to see us, we have our faces veiled.[61] This really eliminates many visits (the purpose our holy Mother had

---

[61] The faces are no longer veiled, as said above, but visits are limited mainly to family members and no more than once a month.

in mind) because it is such a strange experience to talk to a veiled person. Since our life of dedication should keep us separated from all worldly interests, we thank God for these rules of enclosure.

Oh, do not think we hold ourselves so aloof from the world that we have no interest in it. We are interested, intensely interested, in it from one angle—its spiritual needs. We pray for its needs rather than talk about them. We are aware of its problems, and we take them to the only One who can solve them, our dear Lord. We wish to enfold all souls in the mantle of our Immaculate Mother. Your needs and problems have a very special place in my prayers.

Now, please do not worry anymore about my physical well-being. Just keep praying for your little Carmelite as she always prays for you. Jesus, Mary, Joseph protect and bless you.

Your loving daughter,
Sister Marie of the Trinity, D.C.

Letter Thirty-Two

*D*ear Mother, Dad, and all my loved ones,
Pax Christi!

I could hardly wait to write this letter to you. We had the most
thrilling event last week, and I know you will be pleased to hear
every detail of it.

Our dear Sister Mary Genevieve of the Divine Savior pronounced her solemn vows early last Sunday morning. As I have
already told you the details of the profession ceremony, I shall not
go into this description again. It was very impressive, though, to
hear her Charity pronounce the solemn vows *until death* and then
so see the symbol of that death when our Mother Prioress and our
Mother Mistress held the black pall over Sister's prostrate body
during the *Te Deum*.[62]

There are so many wonderful things to tell you that I wrote
notes on the day itself so that I should not forget the beautiful

---

[62] The impressive solemn profession ceremony is now required to
take place during Mass. The faithful are invited to attend. The
sister prostrates during the chanting of the Litany of the Saints as
do priests at their ordination. However, the custom of using the
black pall is no longer in use.

details before writing home. I know you are wondering as were several of us younger novices just what solemn vows mean. Here is a little résumé of the explanation our Mother Mistress gave.

Quoting Abbot Marmion's *Christ the Ideal of the Monk*, her Reverence told us that: "After the Holy Mass, there is no act so pleasing to God as the self-oblation of religious Profession." This applies to the taking of simple vows as well as solemn vows, for in both cases the subsequent acts of the religious have a new value: the added luster of the virtue of religion.

Solemn vows, however, can be compared to the holocaust of the Old Testament in which the victim offered to God was completely destroyed. While simple vows still leave in the individual a link with the world, solemn vows break completely all bonds with the things of time. This may not be too clear. An example helped me to understand better, and I think it will do the same for you.

A person who has made simple vows may possess things as her own, although the use of these possessions is somewhat restricted. On the contrary, one who has made solemn vows cannot possess anything as her own. This example refers to the vow of poverty. In like manner, both the solemn vows of chastity and obedience are a complete oblation and invalidate any act contrary to them.

Our own gloriously reigning Holy Father, Pope Pius XII, issued the Apostolic Constitution *Sponsa Christi* in the Holy Year 1950.[63] Therein, His Holiness advocated the restoration of solemn vows in

---

[63] The Church and Supreme Pontiffs have issued various documents affecting Carmelite life. Most recently, Pope Francis updated *Sponsa Christi* with the Apostolic Constitution *Vultum Dei Quaerere*, which was followed by the related document *Cor Orans* in 2018. As obedient daughters of the Church, the nuns strive to apply these norms laid down by the Holy See while striving to maintain fidelity to our Carmelite charism.

contemplative orders. Hence, Carmels all over the world petitioned to make solemn vows, which petitions were graciously granted.

Our professed sisters made solemn profession on September 14, 1953, the feast of the Exaltation of the Holy Cross. Now as each sister completes the time of probation with the expiration of her temporary vows, her Charity makes solemn profession. After making solemn vows, one is designated as a nun rather than a sister.

In the same Apostolic Constitution, our Holy Father clearly defined the papal (or pontifical) enclosure, which is the counterpart of solemn vows. No one, not even the bishop, may enter the enclosure. In all cases of doctors or workmen who are needed, the care that I described in a previous letter must be taken. Nor may the nuns leave the enclosure except for very grave reasons, and then only with the permission of the Holy See.

Also, in *Sponsa Christi*, our Holy Father encouraged the bishops to restore the ancient rite for the Consecration of Virgins. As this is a pontifical ceremony, only the bishop can perform it. Our bishop has allowed our final professed nuns to have this beautiful consecration, one of the most inspiring rites of the Roman Pontifical. That is the ceremony I witnessed and about which I am so thrilled. Please God you will witness it someday. Meanwhile, would you like to hear a description of it?

The ceremony is built around the Mass and resembles much the rite of Ordination. The bishop having reached the foot of the altar and vested, the Mass began. At the Collect there was added a prayer for the virgin (or virgins). After the Alleluia verse, the bishop having been seated, the archpriest announced to Sister: "Behold the Bridegroom comes! Go forth to meet Him!" What a thrill of joy must have filled her Charity's heart when that message was heard! Then the bishop, having inquired of the archpriest if the virgin was worthy and having received assurance that she was, his

Excellency called three times: "Come!" "Come!" "Come!... I will teach you the fear of the Lord!" Sister Mary Genevieve of the Divine Savior, holding a lighted candle in her right hand, responded and approached. Then she sang the beautiful antiphon: "Receive me, O Lord, according to Thy promises that no injustice may dominate me." It was the plea of the bride for the best gifts of her Beloved.

Sister Mary Genevieve then pronounced the vow of perpetual virginity and expressed her desire to be "blessed, consecrated, and espoused to Our Lord Jesus Christ." As the Litany of the Saints was intoned, the bishop with miter knelt at the foot of the altar. Immediately after the invocation for the faithful departed, his Excellency arose and turned toward the place where Sister had been lying prostrate on the floor since the commencement of the Litany. With crosier in his left hand, the symbol of jurisdiction, his Excellency sang these two invocations:

"That Thou wouldst deign to bless Thy handmaid here present; That Thou wouldst deign to bless and sanctify Thy handmaid here present ..."

to each of which invocation, the Choir responded: "We beseech Thee, hear us!" The Litany was then resumed. At its termination, Sister Mary Genevieve arose, and the bishop intoned the *Veni Creator Spiritus.*

The holy Scapular, white mantle, veil, and crown of flowers were then blessed. After Sister had been clothed with the Scapular and mantle, her Charity chanted the meaningful responsory: "The kingdom of the world and all worldly ornaments have I despised for the love of Our Lord Jesus Christ." Then the bishop chanted the inspiring preface for the Consecration of a Virgin. I wish I could write the whole thing for you to read, but it is too long for that. Just believe me when I tell you that it is one of the most beautiful

things in the Roman Pontifical—comparable to the joyous Exultet of Holy Saturday with which you are acquainted.

Having finished the preface, the bishop again asked of Sister if she were resolved to persevere in holy virginity. Then the black veil was placed on her Charity's head by the bishop in such a way that her face was covered. Meanwhile, his Excellency exhorted her: "Receive the holy veil by which you will be known to have despised the world and to have surrendered yourself to Jesus Christ as spouse." She responded: "He has placed a sign on my forehead in order that I may admit no other lover besides Him." Here is the beautiful explanation of having our faces veiled: Holy Mother Church herself acknowledges this as the sign of our consecration and espousals. Let the world laugh in scorn! We do not care what they say. We are His, and we are happy to show forth our total consecration.

"Receive the crown of virginal excellence ... that you may be crowned by Christ in Heaven," the bishop said as he placed the wreath on Sister's head. More beautiful prayers for her perseverance and sanctification were then said, after which his Excellency pronounced *the curse* on all who would dare to molest her. It is a withering curse that brings out in strong relief the love that Holy Mother Church has for her consecrated virgins.

The Mass was then resumed with the last Alleluia and continued to the Offertory. The bishop, after saying the Offertory verse, received from Sister Mary Genevieve a lighted candle. The host that she was to receive at Holy Communion was then placed on the paten with the Mass host. How her Charity's heart must have vibrated with unspeakable joy when the time of Communion arrived. Can you imagine with what love one would welcome Jesus on that day of days? Just to anticipate this glorious event makes my heart throb with joy.

After the bishop had given the solemn blessing at the end of Mass, he again prayed over the newly consecrated virgin. Then, seated, the bishop presented Sister with the breviary (Office book), saying to her in the name of the Church: "Receive this book, that you may begin the Canonical Hours and read the office in the Church. In the Name of the Father, and of the Son, and of the Holy Spirit. Amen." This is the commission given to the *nun*—to pray publicly in the name of the Church. This is our sacred obligation—our wonderful privilege. The *Te Deum*, the hymn of praise and thanksgiving, having been sung, the last Gospel was read.

Oh, how can mortal tongue ever express the gratitude owed to God for such a privilege as this consecration! Will you pray earnestly that I may be found worthy to become one of these virgins whom St. Methodius has described as "the unbloody altar from which ascends the incense of love"; and we could add through which descends a torrent of graces for souls. Surely Carmel is a powerhouse of prayer. Surely Carmelites are "spiritual ambassadors" before the throne of God.

No doubt you will still hear many disdainful remarks about cloistered nuns, but do not let that bother you. Holy Mother Church loves these consecrated souls among whom Jesus, in His infinite love, allows me to dwell. Thank Him for me always!

Your loving daughter,
Sister Marie of the Trinity, D.C.

Letter Thirty-Three

*D*ear Mother, Dad, and all my loved ones,
   May Christ's peace fill your souls and abide with you always!

Your recent question echoes a similar query in my own mind: "What makes Carmel so austere if there are such joys to be found there; why is it considered such a strict life?" How often I have put that question to myself as I experienced some new joy in this blessed cloister.

There are probably many answers. For one thing, I am sure that not everyone would find the peace and contentment that we find in solitude—in being "completely cut off from the rest of the world." The only real explanation of our satisfaction is the grace of our vocation: we do not yearn for change of scene; we do not wish to see the "latest shows" or to read the "best novels"; we are happy in the environment that others could find only "humdrum and monotonous."

Nevertheless, we do have sacrifices in this matter. For instance, suppose that one of you, Mother, Dad, or any of the children, were to be seriously ill. Faith would enable me to believe that my presence here in Carmel with all its accompanying graces would do you more good than my physical presence with you at home ever could. Yet what suffering there would be in such a separation. We accept this from the very beginning of our life in Carmel, however, since we know that we shall never go home for any such reason.

Other things, too, make our life in spite of all its beauty one of trial. The lack of sleep is a penance for all. It is especially hard during the summer months, when the heat makes sleep almost impossible until the somewhat cooler morning hours. Since the clappers sound at 4:30 a.m. in summer, there is not much time for sleep during those morning hours. Some sisters are so tired that their Charities scarcely know what they are doing. One sister related that her Charity had put both stockings on the same leg and did not discover the error until later.

There are sisters who can be wide awake no matter how early they arise; but at night, their Charities are asleep even when standing. I have actually seen the breviary (Office book) drop on the floor when some poor sister was overcome by sleep at the Divine Office. As one sister aptly put it, we daily whisper, "Dearest Jesus, it is only for *You* that I could get up at this hour day after day!"

The perpetual abstinence and the frequent fasts take their toll on one's strength too. Especially hard is the "black fast" observed each Friday during the greater portion of the year. (Black fast means no milk or egg foods in any form.) Extreme fatigue or a severe headache is the usual counterpart of this observance—but we rejoice to have such a tiny splinter from the Cross on the day dedicated to the memory of our Savior's Passion.

These mortifications, which form only a small part of Carmelite corporal austerities, are felt more keenly because of the manual labor we are bound to do. The injunctions of our holy *Rule*, "You shall do some kind of work that the devil may always find you occupied" and "If any man will not work, neither let him eat," make it clear that our contemplative vocation is not synonymous with an idle life. Some persons have the strange notion that we do nothing all day but stay in the Choir to pray. Oh, we do have many hours devoted to formal prayer each day, but during the remaining hours of the day, we "pray by working."

You would be amazed at the hard work involved in preparing the hosts for Mass: the hours spent standing at the baking machines or cutting the hosts; while counting, packaging, and mailing the orders is but another phase of this work. The work is not burdensome, however, for it is truly a work of love. Each host makes us yearn to receive spiritually our Eucharistic Lord; makes us ardently pray that others will fervently receive Him thus to quench His burning thirst for souls. As we work, we renew our intention of co-offering each Mass that, moment after moment, is begun in some part of the world.

The vestments, altar linens, and other sewing orders keep several sisters constantly concentrating on that exacting work: designing, embroidering, plaiting, and fitting, so that each piece will give glory to our Savior. How wonderful it is to be permitted to prepare, in union with our Blessed Mother, the linens on which Christ is to rest and the vesture that marks the "alter-Christus" as he offers the supreme Sacrifice.

The printing, too, gives ample opportunities for fatigue. Long hours of painstaking work are required to set type so that it is perfect, and then the real work of manipulating the small hand-press begins.

Perhaps this will sound strange, but one of the biggest mortifications along this line is the fact that we always live according to the holy *Rule*. This means that at the sound of the bell, we must lay aside our work and go immediately to whatever exercise the bell summons us. The little St. Thérèse was so perfect in her observance of this point that she would neither finish the word, if writing, nor make one extra stitch, if sewing, after hearing the bell. There is always the temptation to just "finish this little bit."

One of our postulants heard about this punctual obedience and made a resolution to be perfect in its observance. One day, just as her Charity was sweeping the steps, the bell rang. Her Charity hastened to the Novitiate immediately—not even pausing to pick up the dustpan that was in the middle of one step. Thanks be to God, some sister noticed it before anyone could trip over it and fall down the stairs. We received instructions, then, about using "common sense" in our striving for perfection. From this you will see that there are trials—trials that many would find too hard. We who persevere find the joys so great and the opportunities of merit given by these trials so wonderful that we are truly happy. Pray that I may become daily more generous, more ready to "bear all things for and with Christ." You are in my prayers and little sacrifices.

Your loving daughter,
Sister Marie of the Trinity, D.C.

Letter Thirty-Four

*D*ear Mother, Dad, and all my loved ones,
Praised be Jesus Christ!

"*Quid retribuam?* What shall I render in return?" This was the theme of our conferences on our recent "day of recollection." How impressive were the words of Father as his Reverence explained over and over again what we should return to God for the singular grace of a Carmelite vocation. Please thank God with me and for me, at the same time beseeching His grace that your daughter may always be faithful to her vocation.

Worldly people, seeing only the exteriors—the monastery wall, the grate, and the austere cell—conclude that we live a very joyless life. Yet it is the loving acceptance of the sacrifices imposed by our holy *Rule* that creates the peace and happiness that we experience. Detachment is only the negative part in the Carmelite program: the end of our Carmelite austerities is union with God. Our holy Mother so well said, "When love is strong, we desire to give much; when it is perfect, we want to give all." This giving to God is the source of our joy; and the joy, the proof of our vocation.

It is true, as Father so well explained, that unfitness for the life would make it burdensome. Quoting the *Carmelite Directory of the Spiritual Life*, his Reverence said: "It is presumption to push one's self into the religious state without a divine vocation; for only one who is called by God may justly expect to receive the *special* grace needed to fulfill the obligations of this state." He told us, too, that no one, even among seculars, is more unhappy than a person bound to occupations and conditions of life from which he shrinks completely because of his own character and dispositions. How much more true would this be of a cloistered religious.

I guess all of the novices were impressed the same way I was when we listened to Father's clear explanation of how one can know if she really is called to Carmel. Many people wonder how a boy or girl can decide such an all-important question. With the help of an experienced priest who knows something about one's temperament and capabilities, it is not really too hard. The Code of Canon Law gives the three basic signs, which most of us learned in high school religion class: (1) no legal impediment such as an existing marriage vow, etc.; (2) the existence of a good intention, which would exclude anything like desiring to be a religious in order to flee from difficulties in the world or to seek an easy life; and (3) the intellectual, mental, and physical fitness required to bear the obligations of the religious life.

It was this last sign that Father really stressed. It was somewhat of a revelation to me to understand, for the first time, that a really good boy or girl might ardently long to be a Carmelite from very good motives and yet not have a true vocation. Even a genuine desire to embrace all the austerities associated with Carmel in order to prove one's love for God may not be a real sign of a vocation. Father pointed out that many have a somewhat "glamorized" idea of Carmel and hence rush to embrace something that thrills them but that they do not understand.

"I should not like you to be effeminate or even to appear to be that, in any way, my daughters; *I want you to be strong men.*" These are the pointed words that our holy Mother, St. Teresa, has addressed to each of her daughters. We must have enough physical strength to bear the requirements of the holy *Rule* without constantly seeking dispensations. We must have enough intellectual ability to understand the requirements of the vows, and then we must strive to fulfill them.

Most of all, we must have the stamina that keeps us from "going to pieces" over every little thing. Our life of solitude and silence requires healthy nerves. We do not have the relaxing opportunities of change that others enjoy. Ours is a day-in, day-out routine that can be too much for some characters. It is never monotonous for us who, minute by minute, see the Hand of God directing all for our sanctification. Perhaps you smile at my saying this, since I am so young in Carmel. Really, that is how I feel, and how I pray God that I may feel always. It is the expression, in my clumsy language, of what the senior sisters say too.

One final point that Father brought out really startled me. "If novices find things not in accord with their hopes and desires, they have a choice: either they yield or they must go," he said; and then continued, "the order must not yield to the novice but the novice to the Order." You can see how much help we need then to yield perfectly; to overcome gradually the things in our nature that are contrary to the spirit of Carmel. Your prayers are the best help you can give. I want sincerely to be the true Carmelite that Father described in this beautiful way (which is, in reality, a paraphrase of the words of our holy Mother, St. Teresa): "*a devoted friend of Christ,* a loving child of Mary, willing to sacrifice and suffer for them and for souls."

"Many are called, but few are chosen." That was the parting thought Father left with us. Please pray that I may be among the chosen few who persevere in Carmel, for as one saint so beautifully remarked: "If it is hard to live as a religious, it is sweet to die as one!"

Your loving daughter,
Sister Marie of the Trinity, D.C.

Letter Thirty-Five

... many years later ...

$\mathcal{D}$ear Mom and Dad,

How are you? I know that the grandchildren must keep you busy, and I hope they don't tire you out. It was so good to see Sis and her husband and their children when they visited last summer. How they've grown! I look forward to seeing the others next summer. Time flies, and yet your Carmelite feels it was only yesterday that she came to the monastery.

With this letter I have some bittersweet news to share. Our Sister Mary Rose went to her eternal reward after a short battle with cancer. Sister had not been feeling well, so our Mother brought her to the doctor. Alas, the test results revealed that the cancer had returned and with a vengeance.

Sister Rose was as sweet as a rose. She was a hard worker, the kind of person whom everyone could count on. She quietly went about her business and was always there to help another sister in need. A jack-of-all-trades, Sister could cook, sew, garden, and make enrollment cards. We already miss her when we discover a job not done and realize, "Sister Rose always did that!" But what really tests genuine virtue is a difficult illness, such as her cancer. She was such a docile patient, not wanting to give trouble to anyone. Whenever we did something for her, she expressed her gratitude so sincerely. The nuns took turns being with her in the infirmary, praying with her or singing her favorite hymns. Our chaplain came to the infirmary every morning after Mass in order to give her Holy Communion. She also received the Anointing of the Sick, which gave her strength to bear her cross.

Sister Rose's death was a beautiful and peaceful one. The entire community was gathered around her bedside that evening. We prayed the Rosary there and then we prayed Vespers as well, seeing that the end was near. It brings tears of joy to my eyes when I recall that she so peacefully fell asleep in the Lord as we were praying the Magnificat during Vespers. Sister loved the Magnificat and had it printed on her Jubilee card.

Do you remember how I've often quoted a certain saint: "If it is hard to live as a religious, it is sweet to die as one"? Well, after witnessing the holy lives and deaths of nuns in our monastery, I agree it is sweet to die as a religious, but I would say that it is sweet to live as one too. Sister Mary Rose is one of several deaths I've witnessed in Carmel. Each time, I think to myself, "She makes dying look so easy!" This is so consoling for those of us left behind and spurs us to renew our fervor in living our beautiful vocation.

The weather was just perfect for the funeral. The procession moved gracefully down the little road to our cemetery. The bishop and the priests followed the hearse and our entire community took up the rear, all clothed in our white mantles and chanting hymns to Our Lady the whole way. The graveside ceremonies always touch me to tears, especially as we sing the Salve Regina at the conclusion. But a certain peace filled the atmosphere, even as the birds in the nearby woods added their melody.

There is so much more I could write, but time is short. As you know, it is the custom in Carmel to send a short biography of a deceased sister to all the other Carmelite monasteries and to friends and family. I'll send you one when we get that done. Meanwhile, keep Sister Rose and all our deceased sisters in your prayers.

Your loving daughter,
Sister Marie of the Trinity, O.C.D.

Appendix: Daily Schedule

Rise	5:00 a.m.
Morning Prayer (Lauds)	5:30 a.m.
Hour of Prayer	6:00 a.m.
Holy Sacrifice of the Mass	7:00 a.m.
Silent Thanksgiving after Mass (fifteen minutes) followed by Midmorning Prayer (Terce) and breakfast	
Manual Labor	8:30 a.m.
Midday Prayer (Sext) and Examen	10:45 a.m.
Dinner	11:00 a.m.
Recreation	11:55 a.m.
Visit to the Blessed Sacrament	12:55 p.m.
Rest or Free Time	1:00 p.m.
Midafternoon Prayer (None) and Spiritual Reading	2:00 p.m.
Manual Labor	3:00 p.m.
Rosary	4:25 p.m.
Evening Prayer (Vespers)	4:40 p.m.
Hour of Prayer	5:00 p.m.

Supper (or Collation in the Fast)	6:00 p.m.
Recreation	7:00 p.m.
Night Prayer (Compline)	8:00 p.m.
Great Silence/Free Time	8:30 p.m.
Office of Readings (Matins)	9:25 p.m.
Silent Prayer (fifteen minutes)	
Retire	10:00 p.m.

Sophia Institute

Sophia Institute is a nonprofit institution that seeks to nurture the spiritual, moral, and cultural life of souls and to spread the gospel of Christ in conformity with the authentic teachings of the Roman Catholic Church.

Sophia Institute Press fulfills this mission by offering translations, reprints, and new publications that afford readers a rich source of the enduring wisdom of mankind.

Sophia Institute also operates the popular online resource CatholicExchange.com. *Catholic Exchange* provides world news from a Catholic perspective as well as daily devotionals and articles that will help readers to grow in holiness and live a life consistent with the teachings of the Church.

In 2013, Sophia Institute launched Sophia Teachers to renew and rebuild Catholic culture through service to Catholic education. With the goal of nurturing the spiritual, moral, and cultural life of souls, and an abiding respect for the role and work of teachers, we strive to provide materials and programs that are at once enlightening to the mind and ennobling to the heart; faithful and complete, as well as useful and practical.

Sophia Institute gratefully recognizes the Solidarity Association for preserving and encouraging the growth of our apostolate over the course of many years. Without their generous and timely support, this book would not be in your hands.

www.SophiaInstitute.com
www.CatholicExchange.com
www.SophiaTeachers.org

Sophia Institute Press is a registered trademark of Sophia Institute.
Sophia Institute is a tax-exempt institution as defined by the
Internal Revenue Code, Section 501(c)(3). Tax ID 22-2548708.

About the Author

SISTER CLAIRE MARIE OF THE Immaculate Heart, O.C.D. (1925–1996) was a Discalced Carmelite Nun who wrote these letters under the *nom de plume* of Sister Marie of the Trinity. In 1950, as a new Carmelite, Sister Claire Marie was part of the small group of nuns who ventured out from the Carmel in Grand Rapids, Michigan, to found the Carmel of the Holy Cross in Iron Mountain, Michigan. Sister wrote this collection of letters for the diocesan newspaper to explain Carmelite life to the people. In 1957, due to their popularity, the letters were compiled into a book under the title *A Few Lines to Tell You*.